The Hard Way

by

Jeremy Donovan

Dedication

This book is dedicated to my amazing wife, Annie. You have stuck with me through learning *The Hard Way*. I'm grateful for your love and grace. Every day you make me want to be a better man and I love you so very much.

To my daughter, Cadence, and son, Cale; I'm so proud of you and thankful that God gave me such amazing kids. I pray you read this book and never have to learn the hard way.

To my son, Isaiah, I miss you to the point that words cannot explain. I pray that someday we will see each other again.

Acknowledgements

This book would not have been possible without the legendary and amazing author, Norma Jean Lutz. You helped me make my dream come true. (Everyone should Google "Norma Jean Lutz.")

Josh Mayo, who helped me publish this book. You, Josh, are an answer to my prayers. Thank you for being a mentor in this process and an amazing friend and publisher. Please read all of his books, including the latest, *Rehab*. Every one of his books is life changing in its own way.

Others who have played an integral part in my life and this book coming into being: DestinyLife Church, Seven Youth Ministries, Apostolic Teams International, The Sozo Movement, Youth Leaders Coach, Jeanne Mayo's Cadre, Master's Commission USA, Yates Photography, Mercy Seat Ministries, Curvine Music, Josh Mayo Ministries, and the LA and NY Dream Centers.

Thank You

So many people in my life have believed in me, have invested into my life, and never gave up on me. To you I will be eternally grateful:

My wife, Annie, and two sweet children, Cadence and Cale.

My parents, Bill and Rose Donovan.

My brother, Josh, my sister, Sarah, and her husband Thomas Baureis. Thank you for your unconditional love and support.

Thanks to the rest of my family who have been an amazing support in my life, the Kirklands and the Donovans.

To my in-laws, thank you for letting me join your family.

My pastors, mentors, and spiritual parents, Apostles Glenn and Ami Shaffer. You changed my life more than you ever will know. It is an honor to be your son in the Lord.

All the amazing pastors who have poured so much into my life: Tom and Jean Williams, Greg and Beverly Jones, James and Ruby Hutson, Jim and Deretha Bell, Carter and Pam Eby, J.R. and Beverly Damiani, Jaycee and Anna Jennings, Pat and Karen Schatzline, Matthew and Caroline Barnett, Sam and Jeanne Mayo (love you, Mom), and Lloyd and Chris Zeigler (thanks Pastor Z and Mama Chris that you never quit on me). Thank you for believing in me.

Thanks to all the people I call my *best friends,* who I would not want to live life without: Aaron Becker, Gerry and Sadia Blaksley, Cole and Caitlin Zick, Curvine and Candace Brewington, Matt Moore, Hans Hufstetler, Josh and Monica Mayo, Steve and Jessica Robinett, Kyle and Anne Gift, Jeff and Erika Shellenberger, Cliff and Lesa Smith, John and Pam Reed, Richard and Stephanie Blackburn, Gary Wehlacz, Tim and Chrissy Yates, Jonathan and Mattie Cruz, and Randy Bibb.

Thank you to my amazing church family at Destiny Life Church (www.destinylifechurch.tv) and all the students in Destiny Life's Seven Youth Ministries. I love you all.

A special thank you to the mentors and people who got me to where I am in life: Alan and Stacey Blaksley (thank you for adopting me and making me a son), Jeff and Lynné Ray for always being there (even with the late-night emergency phone calls), Paul and Barb Dziedzic, Ted and Debbie Hawley, Ricky and Tish Olivieri, David and Kim Frain, Barb Simpson, Bob and Debbie Diskerud, Jim and Kathy Moore, and Stacey and Tammy Hillis. You are family to Annie and me. We love you all. Thank you for believing in us.

Foreword

Secrets, shame, and guilt cause us to hide. Fearful of not being accepted and frightened that someone will expose hidden sin, many Christians are driven into a false life. From the beginning of the Garden of Eden, man has been hiding behind fig leaves in an attempt to cover up their own shame. Jeremy Donovan strips away any fig leaves left and goes for the only true covering in his new book, *The Hard Way*. He takes a risk along with some bold steps in sharing his personal journey of abuse, shame and guilt in the process of discovering unconditional love.

Raised as a preacher's kid, one might think that these kind of things are not supposed to happen, but tragedy knows no boundaries. From even the first few pages, *The Hard Way* paints a picture of how evil and sin take advantage of any opportunity. No one is exempt. Learning the hard way is a common response, so it is a must read for every parent and teenager. The power of this book is not only in Jeremy's personal story, but in the hope it offers to those who find themselves a victim of some predator or powerless in their own bondage.

Jeremy Donovan came into my life in a providential way. In thirty-one years of pastoring the same church, we had never brought on staff a leader from the outside. Our focus had been, and still is, to raise up leaders within the same spiritual DNA. However, this time was different. We were confident in the knowledge that where we were with the church, God must bring us the right person to serve as our new youth pastor. After nine months of little progress, it happened without effort.

Two years after the launch of a new DestinyLife church campus in the nearby city of Owasso, Oklahoma, we merged with another church and were celebrating our first official Sunday together. On that Sunday, a young man, along with his wife and children, attended as guests. Little did we realize that within months, the Donovans would not only serve on staff with us, but would be part of our own destiny.

I recall one of our leaders saying that Sunday, in passing, "There was a young man in our worship this morning that you may want to meet." The very next day, I found Jeremy's email address on a guest information card and zipped off a quick email, personally welcoming him and his family. An immediate reply came back from Jeremy, "I told my wife Sunday, we have found our church home." Two days later, we discovered ourselves sharing our heart's desires over lunch.

I felt comfortable enough to say that God had promised me spiritual sons in that region. Almost before I could finish my sentence, Jeremy spoke up, "I'm one of those sons." I saw that he meant it as he quickly wiped tears away (maybe hoping I didn't see). Within weeks we found ourselves emerged in a real, divine connection.

Today, Jeremy serves as one of our pastors at DestinyLifeChurch.tv, along with his wife, Annie. They oversee two campuses of youth ministry in Oklahoma and carry a burden for the youth of America.

Jeremy is in his best element when he stands before a high school assembly and speaks out of his experiences. His authority to address these meaningful issues is obvious. He is uniquely qualified to write *The Hard Way.* The lessons he brings from his own brokenness demonstrate the power and need for mentoring. He will be the first to tell you that his journey is still in progress and that we all continue in our walk in health and freedom. This process can be seen in the pages of this powerful story. I count it an honor and blessing to be included in *The Hard Way*.

Glenn Shaffer
Lead Pastor
DestinyLifeChurch.tv

Table of Contents

Introduction

I Had to Learn the Hard Way

My *life sucks!*
Will things ever get any better?
I see no way out of this.

These are statements I've made over myself – droning on and on like a broken record.

Then add to these the things that other people were saying over me.

He'll never learn.

He'll never amount to anything.

He never does anything right.

He just needs to hit rock bottom.

And then the biggie:

He's one who will just have to learn the hard way!

And I did; and I have.

If you have made statements like those above, or if you've ever had these things said about you (and *to you*), then this book is for you.

Even though I cried out time and time again that *my life sucks,* today I can say that is no longer true. Today I am doing things right. I did hit rock bottom with a crash, but I did not lay there and die.

I Needed to Get Back to Normal

When I was in my rut of a destructive lifestyle I looked for books that could help me. My search was futile. All I could find was books on how to be a success in life, or how to find my purpose. That type of book may be ideal for some, but not for me. I needed a book that could help me *get back to normal*. I couldn't find that. The book you are now holding is the book I wished I'd had when my rut was the deepest and my nights were the blackest.

I needed a book that could help me *get back to normal*.

Through the steps outlined in this book (interwoven with many vivid stories) you will find the pathway to true freedom.

You may be reading *The Hard Way* because someone close to you is in a destructive lifestyle. That's great. This book will give you deeper insight as to how you can help that individual.

In this guide you will hear a lot of my story. I want to encourage you before you even start reading – *if I can do it you can to it*.

Ready to Check Out for Good

It was just ten short years ago that I left off from a week-long binge in New York City and headed down the

New Jersey Turnpike towards my home in Philadelphia. I could scarcely see to drive through my blinding tears.

I was screaming out louder than ever before: *My life sucks!*

If you have ever been there, to that point of screaming out through the pain in your life, you know exactly what I'm talking about. I was at the lowest point of desperation. I was deep into cocaine addiction and plagued with depression and anger from which I couldn't break free. Pounding the steering wheel and screaming out to God, "My Life Sucks!" I wished for death to come because that seemed to be the only way to permanently escape the pain.

I drove over the Benjamin Franklin Bridge into Philadelphia and pulled into Old City. This is a part of Philly where historical sites like Independence Hall and the Liberty Bell are located. But there was no independence or liberty for me.

For me Old City provided the clubs and bars that I frequented. Ironically, I grew up as a pastor's kid. But, as you will read, my life took a downhill plunge to rock bottom. I went from being a pastor's kid to a drug-dealing addict.

Because I didn't have the tools to deal with the pain in my life, I found myself in a rut that I couldn't get out of. A rut is simply a grave with the ends kicked out, and I was among the walking dead.

I had arrived in Old City with three hundred dollars in my pocket. I owed way more than that to those who were not the type of people you wanted to be in debt to.

I went to a club where I knew a friend of mine would be more than willing to take my last three hundred dollars in exchange for my drug of choice, cocaine. We went into the restroom where I tried the product and then made the purchase. From there, I drove to my apartment with the full intention of ending it all. I was at rock bottom and saw no way out.

But I hadn't bargained on God's intervention!

In my freezer was a stash of ecstasy that I was supposed to sell. That would be my ticket out of a pain-filled life. I lined out the cocaine on my coffee table and snorted it, then downed as many pills as I could swallow. After that, I turned on the television and waited to die.

But I hadn't bargained on God's intervention!

God's Intervention

I knew God. I knew who He was. I had experienced God many times as a child. I knew there was a call on my life.

As I lay there feeling nothing from all the drugs I put into my system, I heard something. I heard God speak to me. He reminded me that He had called me at a young age.

But I quickly reminded God what a hopeless mess I was. "I've tried to be good before and I even promised that I would change," I told Him. "I'm a screw up who always has to learn the hard way!"

Then God clearly spoke to my heart, "Quit trying and get help."

I got off that couch and called my friend, Cal Seidel. I'd known Cal for a long time. He was one of the few Christians who never gave up on me. I told him what I had done and then I said, "I don't want to die."

What I wanted more than anything at that point, was for God to help me get out of my rut!

He called 911 and within minutes half a dozen cops entered my apartment. I was well-known so my place wasn't hard to find.

It was at this point where God began to show me in an unmistakable way that my prayer was being answered. The cops knew who I was, and yet they believed in me. Rather than charging me with possession, they charged me with "being a harm to myself."

They loaded me into an ambulance and drove me to the local hospital which I knew well. (I'd been there often.) They pumped my stomach full of charcoal. I can list many reasons why I will never do drugs again; getting my stomach pumped is among the top five. A horrific experience.

Norristown Building 50

After a few days in the hospital the cops came to my room and said they were moving me to a new hospital where I would receive more help. I had no idea until they pulled into the gates that I was entering one of the worst places imaginable – Norristown Building 50.

I had been admitted to mental institutions before, but they were privately owned and were actually kind of nice. Building 50 was an extension of the city jail where they took all the crazies. This definitely became rock bottom for me.

I knew this was not how I wanted to live. It was time to stop learning the hard way. It was time to stop screaming out in uncontrollable rage, begging God to take me out of my misery. I knew life could be better, full of joy, hope and promise.

I remember one time sitting in the park with my baby son, Isaiah, and watching the other families. (Yes, I was a teen father at age nineteen. More about that later in the book.) They appeared so full of happiness and I had so little. I never had custody of my son, but for the first two years, his mother tried to give me a chance at being a father. A park was located near where she and Isaiah lived and I liked to take him there. I would watch with amazement, wondering how other people could be so happy.

From the Darkness into the Light

After a few months in Building 50 – which seemed like years – I was released to a rehab in West Palm Beach, Florida. I went from being locked up and not seeing the light of day for months, to basking in the sunshine on the beach at one of the best rehabs in the country. God was doing what He promised. I put it in His hands and He was guiding me.

Climbing out of my rut to recovery was not easy. It required tools and steps that I've learned along the way.

The Hard Way is a book you will want keep with you as you walk through the process of getting out of your rut, to use as a reference guide. In this book, you'll learn from the experiences of one who has been there, who has come out, who has survived – and who is now thriving!

Truly Alive

Today I'm a youth pastor. I'm married to my beautiful wife, Annie, and we have two wonderful children. My life counts for something. I no longer have to do things the hard way.

Today I can say, "Life is amazing and I am no longer among the walking dead. I am truly alive!"

If I can say it, I know you can.

CHAPTER 1

The Diagnosis

Packing Bacon

In 1998, I was twenty years old and living in Philadelphia where I'd spent most of my life. I had only recently learned that I was a teen father, which was a shock. I was able to find a job in a meat packing plant. If you've never been around the smells and sounds of a meat packing plant, all I can tell you is that it's not a nice place to spend twelve hours a day.

This was a few months before I hit rock bottom the final time, as I described in the introduction. I showed up for work at four in the morning. I was on the production line in a walk-in refrigerator in the basement of the plant. I packaged bacon for twelve long, endless, boring hours each day. The repetition was enough to drive anyone insane. I can still hear the sound of the machine that sealed the packages – banging over and over and over again. This was a tough job for a dreamer who had his heart set on making something of himself.

Meanwhile, I was drinking daily, getting deeper into drugs, and was an absentee father. Yes, I was a dreamer, but at the same time I was making a mess of everything.

The Headaches

At this same time, I started to get severe headaches that were so excruciating that when they hit all I could do was curl up in a ball and cry until I fell asleep. This didn't help me in life. They would hit me at any part of the day and no medicine worked to relieve the pain.

At this point in my life, most of the people who knew me viewed me as a total screw up. My parents who loved me dearly lived about 5,000 miles away in Anchorage, Alaska. I felt totally alone and isolated. My life consisted of headaches, packing bacon, and sleeping on couches at anyone's house who would let me stay for a few weeks. I was basically homeless.

Add to that the self-medication of drinking, drugs and anything else that could take my mind off the endless rut in which I was stuck. No wonder I found myself screaming, "My life sucks!"

I told people about my headaches and they seemed to think I was exaggerating. Some said it was from all the junk I was putting into my body. No matter; I knew they were real and excruciatingly painful. I just tried to steel myself and live through them.

Isn't this what many of us do in our lives? We know there's something wrong, but instead of diagnosing it, we just try to live with it. This is a quick road to that boulder – that place we call *rock bottom*. If you realize there is something going wrong in your life that is causing you pain (or causing pain for those you love), it's time to stop and diagnose it. Don't wait.

Hit My Boulder

I hit my boulder on a Friday, just after my 21st birthday. I was walking in Montgomeryville Mall, looking to buy something for my girlfriend. I could feel one of the headaches coming on. I knew it was going to be a bad one, so I decided to cut my shopping short and get out of the mall. I walked as fast as I could but before I reached the doors, the headache hit and I passed out. After what seemed to me just a few seconds, I woke up in a puddle of my own vomit, a security guard standing over me.

The guard said he saw me faint and asked me how I felt. Ever the tough guy, I told him I was fine. Totally embarrassed, I stood up and left the mall. When I got to my car, the headache hit full force again. I passed out again. When I woke up, it was almost dark, so I'd been unconscious for several hours. As before, I woke up in my own vomit.

That settled it! Finally, I had the good sense to get diagnosed and drove myself to the nearest hospital. When I told my story to the nurse in the emergency room, she immediately rushed me into the back. In a few short minutes, I was being rolled into a room for a CT Scan. After the CT

Scan, I was placed in a room where I was able to call my dad and mom to tell them I was in the emergency room.

While I was on the phone with my parents, the doctor came in the room. I'll never forget the look in his eyes. I never before remember seeing a doctor who was scared, but this one looked scared.

The first step in getting out of the rut lifestyle –
acknowledge something is wrong and that
you may need help.

"Jeremy," he said, "I don't know how you can be talking to me right now. You have a cerebral brain aneurysm that has burst. Your brain is currently bleeding."

Later I learned that only one in three people live through a brain aneurysm. If it bursts, that statistic gets worse and mine had been bleeding for hours now. I was rushed into surgery as my parents raced to a plane, wondering if I would be alive when they got to Philadelphia.

Get Honest; Get Help

Today, as I look back on this entire scene, I realize that I could have avoided the entire disaster if had just stopped, gotten honest with myself, acknowledged something was wrong, and then followed through with a proper diagnosis.

This is the first big step in getting out of the rut lifestyle. You have to acknowledge something is wrong and that you may need help. This can be difficult to do. You will have some people who will never believe in you. Even when you admit something is wrong and you need help, they may laugh at you and call you a screw up.

You may have friends who are also in the *rut lifestyle* of learning the hard way. They don't want to be in their misery rut alone, so they'll tell you there's nothing wrong and that you're fine. No matter what anyone says, your first step is to diagnose your issues.

King David Learned the Hard Way

King David from the Bible understood this concept of learning the hard way. Second Samuel 11:1 sets the scene.

In the spring, at the time when kings go off to war, David sent Joab out with the king's men and the whole Israelite army. They destroyed the Ammonites and besieged Rabbah. But David remained in Jerusalem.

It was springtime and kingdom business needed to be taken care of, but the king, David, sent his men to do the work instead. He stayed home.

Now King David was a man chosen of God, but he was also a man who seemed to get stuck in ruts of having to learn the hard way.

At this point in his life, David had been king for a number of years. Things were going well in his life. It had been a difficult road to get where he was. Giants and kings had tried to keep him from his destiny, but nothing would keep

David from the call God had on his life. He honored his king even when his king tried to kill him. So God blessed him with the kingdom.

Just as things were looking good, it happened – David came to a fork in the road. He came to a point where he needed to diagnose himself and his situation. It was a time when he could have and should have listened to the wisdom of God and the wisdom of his close counselors. He did not stop and he did not diagnose – a sure sign of someone who will have to learn the hard way.

What was his fork in the road? (It's different for everyone.) For him it was smoking hot, beautiful Bathsheba who lived right next door. He saw her bathing on her rooftop and he wanted her. King David took a wrong turn – the one that led right into his rut and soon he would hit that boulder face first. King David was supposed to go to war and lead his men, but instead, he made the wrong choice and stayed home.

King David wanted her so bad that he sent for her that moment. The boulder would hit later, when he learned Bathsheba was pregnant. Now what could he do? Her husband, a loyal military man, was out fighting battles.

Even now, if King David had stopped and diagnosed the situation, he would have realized that he was on the route to being someone who was in a rut of making a series of wrong decisions. But he didn't stop.

The next step was to get rid of the husband. So King David ordered her husband to be placed on the front lines of war so he would be killed in battle. Now his sin of adultery was compounded by murder.

King David knew his God. He knew these actions were not right, but he was in a rut.

Stop and Diagnose

Does this sound like your life? You see the signs, but you keep going and keep multiplying and compounding the wrong actions and bad decisions?

If you see the signs and you don't stop and change, rock bottom could kill you. As I walked around with my headaches, I knew something was wrong but I didn't want to see it. People kept telling me it was no big deal and I believed them.

> If you see the signs and you don't stop and change, rock bottom could kill you.

If you know something is wrong, even if people tell you it's no big deal, remember it's *your* life. Stop and diagnose the problem or the boulder may hit.

I realize now that I am SO fortunate to be alive after suffering from a brain aneurism. I look back and realize now that I should have gotten my headaches diagnosed much sooner than I did. Perhaps then I wouldn't have had to walk through everything I did.

The first step is to admit the fact that you are someone in the school of hard knocks; you have to learn the hard way. Believe me, when you do you will find those who are willing to stand by you.

The most important One that I found was God. It was amazing how far away He seemed all the time I was running away. But the moment I admitted that I was face first in the boulder of rock bottom; the moment I admitted that I had a destructive habit of learning things the hard way; the moment that I admitted that I desperately needed help, I turned around and there He was! God was right there for me and ready to walk with me.

If you are that someone who always has to learn the hard way, I hope you will stop right now and diagnose your problem.

Yours may be a general admission, "I always have to learn things the hard way and I don't want to do that anymore."

Or perhaps you are just now entering into a dangerous rut – or you are already deep into that rut. This might be things like hate, anger, bitterness, lying. Or perhaps your rut is drugs, alcohol, pornography or sex addiction. It could be any combination of several of the above and plenty more you can name.

It May Be a Good Spot

I hope you're starting to get it now. The hard way is not the way to go. It's, well, *hard*. Even when things seem fun and you're *getting away with it,* that boulder can come and take you out.

Stop for a moment and think about your situation. Before you go any further in reading this book, stop and diagnose yourself. Look over the situations and choices in your life. Reflect on who you are and where you are. Do you like what you see?

If you are in a "my life sucks" moment right now, then you may be one of those who always has to learn the hard way. Ironically, you may be in a good spot – especially if it makes you stop and assess.

Can you look back over your life and remember times and places where caring people tried to tell you that you were on the wrong path, yet you still kept going down the same way? You are definitely in the *hard way* category.

It's no accident that you are reading this book. Hopefully you are ready to diagnose your situation and your circumstances and you are ready to make the needed changes.

Let me warn you though. If you see the signs and you don't stop and change, hitting rock bottom could ruin you. As I walked around with my headaches I knew something was wrong but I didn't want to see it. It very nearly killed me.

Right this moment, you can stop, pray, and ask God to search your heart. Then ask Him to help you change, and *show you how to change*. He is faithful and He will answer that prayer. As the Lord helps you to diagnosis your problem(s), be sure to write them down. Then you can be even more specific in your diagnosis.

CHAPTER 2

The Father's Love

My Father God Loves Me More

Growing up, I was fortunate to experience the true love of a father. My dad is an amazing father who loved me unconditionally. No matter what I did, I always knew he loved me. He demonstrated God's love to me in a very real way.

Since I have become a father, I can now understand to an even deeper level what *father love* is all about. My daughter, Cadence, and my two sons, Isaiah and Cale, are so important to me in my life.

Every day, I pray that I may see Isaiah again, and I treasure every moment that I have to share with Cadence and Cale.

As a father, I realize that there is nothing my kids can ever do that would make me stop loving them. In other words, I will never love them any less because of their actions. Likewise, they can't do anything that would make me love them more, because I already love them deeply – to the point of laying down my own life for them.

Obviously, there are times when I may not be *happy with their actions,* but they can't do anything that would make me love them any less. I love them so much more than I could ever describe in words in this book.

Then I am overcome with the knowledge that as much as I love my children, my Father God loves me even more. Everything He has done for me is due to His unfailing, unconditional love. And that unconditional love extends to every human being – even to you.

We Deserve the Wages of Sin

We are all sinners who have done nothing to deserve God's love. In fact, we did everything to deserve the wages of sin, which the Bible confirms is death (Romans 6:23). God sent His only Son to die on the cross in one of the most painful ways of death possible. He sent His only Son to take all of our sins upon Him and pay the price for us. He did this for us because He loves us. God did this to set us free and give us the opportunity to be His sons and daughters.

Now I love a lot of people, and there are many wonderful people in my life that I am thankful for. But as much as I love my friends and even family, there is no way I could ever send one of my children to die for them.

God did this for us – even those of us who rejected Him. This is so important to understand as you come out of your rut. God sees you and He knows you are a mess, and yet He sent His son to die for you.

He doesn't love you because of what you do; He loves you because of who He is. God IS love (1 John 4:8b)! When you accept Jesus as Lord of your life, He comes into your life and you become His child. You don't have to worry about messing up on your way out of your rut. There's nothing you can do that will ever remove you from your Father's love.

A Lie of the Enemy

When I was a little child, I had a horrible fear that if I messed up, God would withdraw His love from me. I'm not sure where that thought came from, but it was a lie that the enemy used against me more than once.

To this day, I can remember specific moments when I was so hard on myself because I believed God stopped loving me over something I had done. This thought pattern became so entrenched, it followed me well into my adult life.

The condemnation I suffered under disarmed me and consequently I had no will to fight off temptation. I felt condemned, not by God but by the way I *perceived* He felt about me.

Our perception of God can be the deciding factor as to whether or not we stay in a rut. I perceived Him as a father who removed his love from me every time I messed up. This led me to believe I had to get saved all over again each time I made a mistake or messed up.

Our perception of God can be the deciding factor as to whether or not we stay in a rut.

Many times, I sat alone and cried out to God, begging Him to please let me be close to Him again. My perception of a condemning father almost drove me nuts.

"I Thought You Paid..."

The first time I felt this in a deep way, I was only about six years old, but I remember the details as though it happened yesterday. I was staying the night at my friend Jamie's house. He was a few years older than me but we were best buds for quite a few years growing up. We were hanging out during the day and decided to go to the corner store and get some penny candy. (Yes, I'm old enough to have purchased penny candy at the corner store – before Wal-Mart and convenience stores.)

I picked out a few Tootsie Rolls because those were my favorite. I assumed Jamie was paying for my candy so I just proceeded out of the store. When we were outside eating our candy, Jamie asked me why I had not paid for mine. My heart sank into my stomach as I said, "I thought you paid for them."

He replied, "Nope. I just paid for mine." Then he started laughing.

I was devastated. I had just broken one of the Ten Commandments. I had stolen! I was too embarrassed to go back to the store and confess my mistake.

I remember lying in my bed that night, crying and thinking God didn't love me anymore because I had broken the commandment, "Thou shall not steal." I prayed and ask Him to forgive me of my sins, but I went right on condemning myself.

As I look back now, I realize how crazy that was. I had not intentionally stolen anything. I was a small child and I sincerely thought my friend Jamie had paid for my Tootsie Rolls.

For months after, while riding in my parents' car, when we would drive by that store, an overwhelming guilt would wash over me, reminding me of my awful sin. To this day, I remember the feelings of guilt and condemnation I felt through that situation. I remember it also because I have felt it many times since.

Today that store is gone, but if it were still there, I would go in and pay for those Tootsie Rolls.

The truth is, God forgave me the moment I prayed and asked for forgiveness. It wasn't God condemning me for stealing the candy, it was me. I was doing it to myself. The Bible says, "He remembers your sin no more" (Hebrews 8:12). If He doesn't remember them, He can't remind you of them. Think about it, why would God condemn us for sins that He sent His Son to pay for? God forgives us of our sins; all we have to do is ask.

A Natural Born Salesman

I have learned more and more about the Father's love in recent years, and I am growing in my faith walk. I'm also learning how that voice of *condemnation* continually tries to creep in and mess up my thinking, even today.

Here's a case in point. During my years in ministry, I have continually heard admonitions that we should not be self-promoters. I was told, "God doesn't bless a self-promoter in ministry. God is the promoter of those who deserve it."

I'm sure this is true, but at the same time, it was very confusing to me because I'm a natural born salesman. I couldn't figure out how to network and not self promote. It all appeared to be the same to me.

This came to a head recently when I had the opportunity to attend an event attended by some of the top pastors in the nation. I admit I was quite nervous. Because of my somewhat checkered past, I'm still a little more comfortable around street people than I am around a room full of pastors. But in spite of that, I wanted to network and make new friends. So that night at that event, I walked around and tried to make friends. Meanwhile, over and over in my mind I was telling myself, "Don't sell yourself; don't self promote. If you do, God won't bless you in ministry with these friendships. They will reject you."

Of course these thoughts made me even more nervous. As I left, I was thinking, "Everyone there must have thought I was stupid. I must have looked like an idiot."

On my drive home that night, I repented to God, saying things like, "God I'm so sorry if I did anything that even closely resembled self-promotion. I totally understand if I did and you don't allow me to create relationships with those people."

Once again, I was like that little boy who lay in bed beating himself up for inadvertently failing to pay for penny candy. The condemnation was the same. My perception was this: *In spite of the fact that my Father God loved me and sent Jesus to die for my sins, He still gives ultimatums.*

In other words, I was thinking, *If I do thus and so, then God won't bless me.* Or *He won't love me anymore.* This is not a true representation of the love of the Father and it is not true. God does *not* give ultimatums.

God Loves You Right Where You Are

A few days after the experience at the event with the room full of pastors, I was sitting at a restaurant with one of my pastor mentors, Greg Jones. I explained to him the struggle I experienced with not wanting to self promote.

I will never forget the look on his face when he realized I had not yet grasped the fullness of God's grace and love.

Pastor Greg said to me, "Jeremy, God loves you so much; even if you *did* make the mistake of self promotion, He wouldn't take away your friendships or your ministry. He loves you right where you are and He will get you right where you need to be."

Isn't it amazing how one little seed of truth can cut right through the darkness of the lies and deception of the enemy? Pastor Greg's answer was so simple and yet so profound. It set me free.

You may not be dealing with this same type of thinking, but many people believe that God gives ultimatums. Like me, they believe if they do this or that (or fail to do this or that); God will not love them anymore – or that He will never bless them.

It is such a relief to know how much your Father God loves you. When you grasp this truth it will be a huge step toward getting out of your rut. These thoughts of condemnation cause us to focus on ourselves – on what WE are doing or not doing. The key is to focus on the immense and all-encompassing love of the Father God.

A Twenty-Million Dollar Contract

In 1990, Darryl Strawberry was signed to the Los Angeles Dodgers for a five-year, twenty-million dollar contract. When Darryl Strawberry arrived to play ball for this team, some of his teammates led him to the Lord.

In the three years that followed, Darryl became suicidal. He drank more and was arrested for beating his wife. His life was in a downward spiral as he continued to be a candidate for rehab.

Darryl once commented that when he found God, he began to look at everything he had to do as a Christian and it seemed too difficult to attain.

By 1994, Darryl Strawberry did not show up for a Dodgers' exhibition game and they decided to let him go. The Dodgers had paid twenty million dollars for Darryl

Strawberry to come and win the World Series for them. Four years later they paid him three million dollars just to go away.

I have never met Darryl Strawberry personally. I'm sure he is a good person. I do know that he was one of my favorite baseball players when I was a kid. He was obviously in a rut, and being a person who has experienced my own fair share of ruts, I can say with some certainty that Darryl simply failed to grasp the full scope of the love of the Father. It appears that Darryl Strawberry concentrated on what *he was unable to do in his own strength*. Somehow he perceived God as the harsh lawgiver who demands perfection.

Perhaps like me, Darryl believed that every time he messed up, God no longer loved him. And also like me, a big part of his rut was his lack of understanding the love of the Father.

You Have to Get Up

Many people believe that if they mess up, it's all over – it means they have to start all over again with God. This is simply not true. You don't have to start over; you just have to *get up!*

I can't say it enough – God loves you right where you are; and he doesn't give you ultimatums. Even when you think you have messed up so badly that there is no hope of ever getting better, God still believes in you and He still loves you.

Don't quit; don't give up. With God's help, you will get out of your rut and you will find greatness. Don't concentrate on your problems; concentrate on God's love for you and learn about the tools He has provided for you to get out of your rut.

Don't quit; don't give up. With God's help you will get out of your rut and you will find greatness.

Will you fall along the way? Perhaps. But with God by your side, you will not *fail*. God loves you and He will walk with you through it all. He will make you what you are supposed to be. He will give you greatness that you can only dream of from the bottom of a rut. He loves you that much. He doesn't want you to stay in your rut. He sees GREATNESS in you. You need Him to help you get through this and He's right there for you!

CHAPTER 3

Healing from the Past

Healing the Past

After the diagnosis for my brain aneurysm, the doctors set up a plan for surgery and then a plan for my recovery process.

Our life problems are the same way. Once we acknowledge their existence, we must make a plan for healing and recovery. The doctors who took care of my aneurysm were dealing with fixing what had already happened. In the same way, in order for you to get better you have to fix the past. This idea works for anything in life.

As I mentioned before, I can vividly remember sitting in *Norristown Building 50* only a few short years after my aneurysm. When I first arrived, they locked me in a room all alone and it scared me out of my wits. It was a padded room and completely white. There was only a rubbery red chair in the corner and a light in the ceiling protected by bars so you could not get to it.

I sat in that room hour after endless hour. I had been off drugs for a few days so my mind did not have the medication I had trained it to love so well. This meant I was no longer numbing my mind. It was working free and clear.

I had plenty of time to think. There were no windows to look out of, no scenery to gaze at. Nothing to look at but stark white walls and one lone chair. Carved in that one lone chair were three words. Placed there obviously by some hapless victim who had gone on before me. It simply said: "GOD IS FAKE."

It simply said: "GOD IS FAKE."

I sat there reading it over and over again. I began to pray to God and as I did, He began to speak to me and take me on a journey that proved to me beyond the shadow of a doubt that those three words could not have been more wrong.

Reading the Bible

The first part of my journey was healing from my past. Like I said at the beginning of this chapter, going back and fixing what has already happened is the first step.

While I was institutionalized, a preacher came to visit me. Because he brought me a pack of cigarettes, I let him talk to me. He was the first person I remember during this time who demonstrated the love of Jesus. He also brought me a Bible to read. Since I had nothing else to do, I read that Bible.

I had never felt so close to God in my life. He met me where I was. (He will meet you where you are.) I continued to pray that He would help me get out of there. I desperately wanted to try this thing that others called *life*. That thing that I seemed to have messed up in a big way.

To the Rehab Center

Finally, the judge allowed my release if I agreed to go to a rehab center in Florida, a place called, *Behavioral Health of the Palm Beaches*. It seemed that Florida has different laws than the rest of the country when it comes to long-term treatment. It is one of the few states that allows extended care and insurance coverage for it.

Once the decision came down, I was released to a friend Ricky Olivieri. He escorted me to the airport and then to Florida. I'll never forget that ride. It was the first time I had felt even *semi*-free for many months.

After a short flight to West Palm Beach, Florida, I found myself in a beautiful apartment on the beach in Florida. The comparison between this new place and a padded cell cannot be described.

I felt as though I hadn't slept in months. While I was in the mental ward, I was locked in a cell with about ten other guys at night. All I can say is they were not the nicest guys in the world. As a result I learned to sleep very lightly;

always on guard so no one would hurt me or rape me. Rumor had it these brutal acts were common in such cells.

Close to Heaven

When I arrived at rehab, they checked me in. I did not have to go through the typical detox process because I'd been in the mental ward so long my system was free of drugs. So they gave me my own room with a full-sized bed, and a key! My room door had a lock on it that *locked people out.* I was no longer locked in.

I remember thinking that this must be heaven – or very close to it.

I closed the door, locked it securely, and went into what was possibly the deepest sleep I have ever had. I still look back at that night and remember it as the best night's sleep I had had in many years.

The next morning I woke up to see a huge black man standing over me. In that brief moment my feeling of safety and comfort flew right out the window. *Does this guy have a key to get into all the rooms?*

He looked straight at me and said, "Has anyone told you today that they love you?"

Confused, I sputtered, "Nope."

"Well, I do," he replied, "and Jesus does too."

I started laughing, "You don't even know my name."

"I know your name, Jeremy. I work here, Dog. I've got your chart. Now get up and make that bed."

The man's name was Jarrod and he was a guard/orderly. Every morning of those first few weeks, the same scene was repeated. Jarrod would wake me up by saying, "Has anyone told you today that they love you?"

I would always reply, "No."

Then he would say, "Well I do and Jesus does too. Now get up and make that bed." In the days to come, Jarrod helped me more than the counselors ever could.

As an orderly, Jarrod didn't have to reach out to me, but he did. He loved me and helped me through my mess even though he didn't have to.

Dissecting My Past

I was also blessed that this rehab center had a Christian study course that I could enter. Of course I did it; I knew God had called me into the ministry. I later learned it is the only rehab center on the east coast that offers such a course of study.

As I spent time in counseling and began feeling more and more comfortable at the center, I realized that the staff genuinely wanted to help set me free from this *hard way* life I had been living. So again, I had to diagnose that this described me and admit I needed help. Once I did that, it was time to start getting to the work of dissecting my past.

This meant bringing up and confronting a painful memory from my past that I had fought with and suppressed for over ten years. I finally opened up to face some things I that I had never shared with anyone.

At the age of nine, I entered into several years of intense confusion and pain in my life. I came to learn that this incident formed the impetus for many of my actions later on in my life.

From a Happy Child to an Angry Teenager

Every year when I was a child, our family went to visit my grandparents for holidays like Thanksgiving and Christmas and a few weeks in the summer. They lived near Cleveland.

It was the year I turned nine – that Thanksgiving – I remember vividly. Like always, we traveled to my grand-parents' and a boy who was connected to our family was also there. (I will omit the details from this book because I have forgiven him. I'll just call him John.)

That year was just as I had always remembered it, espe-cially the amazing aromas of food cooking at my grand-parents' restaurant. The name of their restaurant was the Fiesta, even though there wasn't one Mexican dish on the menu. One half of the Fiesta was a restaurant where fami-lies came to eat. The other half was a bar that served as the *watering hole* for the locals. As a kid, to me this was the coolest place in the world. I would go into the bar and eat candy from the candy shelf and talk to all my Grandpa's friends and customers. To top it off, we could order what-ever we wanted off the restaurant menu for free.

Grandpa and Grandma lived in the apartment above the restaurant. It was such an awesome place! Needless to day, I loved our visits there.

This one night the restaurant was to close down early. I could hear the sounds downstairs as the last of the people left the bar. I had fallen asleep in the living room area. Halfway through the night, I was awakened by John. He was about fifteen at the time. He began to molest me that night. I knew it was wrong but I so looked up to this older boy and I didn't want to cross him so I went along with it. This went on for hours that night with details I will not get into.

Once he started this pattern of behavior, it continued until I was almost eleven. Every Christmas, Thanksgiving and summer would bring this pain. I began to hate this boy and everyone around me, because I so dreaded each and every visit to my grandparents' home. A memory that had once been filled with joy and happiness was now forever tainted and spoiled.

From that point, I went from being a happy child who enjoyed an almost storybook childhood to being an angry teenager. I remember people in my church asking why I acted certain ways. No one could understand why I was so angry and out of control.

Masking the Pain

Around the age of thirteen, my world opened up to alcohol and other ways to self-medicate. I was hurt and angry and did not realize that I was seeking any way possible to mask the awful pain. Not only had I been violated, but as a child, I felt I had been betrayed.

From there my life spiraled downhill quickly. Before my senior year in high school, my parents had moved me as far away from Philadelphia as possible – Anchorage, Alaska.

By that time, I was a full-blown druggy. I had started with alcohol and then moved to weed, acid, ecstasy, and Special K. On the streets, I was what they call a *garbage head* – someone who would do anything to alter their state of being sober. By my senior year, I had had multiple sex partners. I slept with as many girls that would let me. I projected my inner pain to hurting them. It's so true that hurting people are the ones who tend to hurt people. My life personified that adage.

On the streets, I was what they call a *garbage head* – someone who would do anything to alter their state of being sober.

Sleeping with multiple girls was also my way of proving I wasn't gay. Of course, the ultimate irony is that all of the things I was doing were fun. That's the craziest thing about learning the hard way. Most things you do can be fun. But the Bible is so right when it says that fun is only for a season (Hebrews 11:25). The truth was, I was headed directly into a very deep rut and I didn't see the boulders at rock bottom. But man, they were coming at me, hard and fast.

In my senior year I got a girl pregnant and I was going to be a father. She was my high school sweetheart, but she had no idea what she was getting into when she got hooked up with me.

Thank You, Dan

One of the things I did right was that I graduated from high school. My dad made sure of that – with a little help from a school security guard named Dan.

Dan is a guy I came to know well at my high school. He went above the call of duty when it came to me. I was flunking out of my senior year. No surprise there. I found how easy it was to get mixed up with the wrong crowd – no matter where I lived. Alaska was no different than Philadelphia!

In Alaska I was introduced to cocaine. I began working for, and partying with, a Dominican family there. They had some of the best drugs in the city. I had not been seen for days, but somehow Dan found out where I was. He knew me and Linky well. Linky was my friend's *street name*. I had been staying at Linky's house and we'd been on a binge for days. Dan arrived at the house and busted it up like he was John Wayne.

He grabbed us both and said, "You two are walking across that stage on graduation night, whether you do it yourself or I drag you."

Let me say right here and now to Dan from Service High School in Anchorage, Alaska – as angry as I was at you on that day – a big heartfelt, ***Thank You.***

A Hurting Person With Issues

My high school sweetheart was back in the Philadelphia area. She had gotten pregnant during a visit I made there over Christmas break. (By the way, this was a trip my parents and many other people had advised me not to make. As usual, I had to learn the hard way.)

After graduation, I had nothing to do, so I thought I belonged back in Philadelphia. I packed up and went back. My son, Isaiah, was born on my nineteenth birthday.

I started working at a pork plant during the day and spent my nights working in the city at nightclubs, dealing drugs. I did many stupid things during this time, and even worse, I did mean things. I was a hurting person who had not dealt with the issues that haunted me from my past.

One night during a party at my house, I was drunk and high beyond words. The girl that was with me left crying, saying that I was the meanest person she had ever met.

I went from screaming at her to stripping off all my clothes and climbing up a tree with a rope around my neck. When I got to the top, I tied the other end to the tree and began screaming at all the people at the party. A scene like this gives a pretty clear indication that I was more than a little messed up. But it all started with me not dealing with my past – the anger at having been molested as a kid.

For you to find your way out of your rut, you must find healing from your past. That's what happened to me. At the *Behavioral Health of the Palm Beaches,* I finally opened up and talked about the awful memories, and as I did I became horribly angry.

The Day It All Broke

One morning it all broke. I fell to the floor in the fetal position and began to cry. I hadn't cried like that in many,

many years. I had cried tears of anger in the past few years, and even tears of hopelessness. But this was different; I was sad. It was almost like a *healing* cry.

In the middle of my cry, Jarrod walked into my room and changed my life forever. He came in to say his daily line: "Has anyone told you they love you today?" but he stopped when he saw me lying there. He asked me what was going on and I told him the whole story. He was the first person outside of a counselor that I had ever told. He then proceeded to tell me the story of Blind Bartimaeus (Mark 10:46-52).

Blind Bartimaeus

Jesus had come to the city of Jericho. As He and His disciples were leaving the city, a large crowd followed. A blind man was sitting by the side of the road whose name was Bartimaeus. This blind man cried out, "Jesus, Son of David, have mercy on me!"

The crowd heard him yelling and told him to shut up. They didn't want the crazy blind man to bother Jesus. But Bartimaeus didn't care; he cried out even louder, "Jesus, Son of David, have mercy on me."

Jesus heard him crying out and stopped and said "Call him over here." So the crowd, probably annoyed with the man, told him, "You got your way – he's calling for you." The Bible says in Mark 10:50, "He stood up, threw off his cloak and ran to Jesus."

Cry for Help

Jarrod then explained to me what it was that Bartimaeus did to get healed. The first thing he did was cry out for help.

When you need healing from your past, a big thing you must do is find people to help you. They won't seek you out, you have to find them. You have to cry out to Jesus most importantly. But you need to find others to help you as well, such as counselors, pastors and friends who are Christians.

I say to cry out to Jesus first, because it's important that He guide you to the right people. There are many well-meaning people with titles to their names, but that doesn't necessarily mean they are the right people to help you, or even that they are the best equipped.

Sometimes it's not even their fault. On my journey, I came into contact with pastors and counselors who said things that were more hurtful than constructive. I know now that they didn't mean to hurt me. I'm sure they had my best interest at heart. They simply didn't know any better. They were doing the best they knew how.

To be fully healed from your past, you cannot do it alone. You need Jesus and you need people who know how to hear from Him. AMEN↓

Stop Caring What Others Think

The second thing Jarrod showed me from this story is that, in order to get healed from your past, you have to stop caring what other people think. Many of us are so worried about what others think, or that they will find out who we *really* are, that we never cry out for help.

In his book *Extraordinary,* John Bevere says, "You will serve whom you fear." What he is saying is if you fear what people think then you will do what you believe they want. But if you fear God, you will do what you believe He wants. God definitely wants you to find healing from your past.

I could no longer worry about what people would think of me. I had to let it out and work through it.

Give Up Your *Rights*

The third thing Jarrod taught me is based in verse 50, where it says, "He threw off his cloak and ran to Jesus." This is the part of healing and recovery that most people miss as they read this passage. Jarrod explained to me that this blind man's cloak was very important.

In Bible times, the color of a person's cloak meant something. There was a special cloak that was required in order to be a beggar on the streets of Jericho. For Bartimaeus, to be a blind beggar, he had to go before the courts of Jericho and prove he was blind. Only after he proved this could he get his cloak or his *right to beg.*

So when Jesus called Bartimaeus to come to him to receive his healing, before Bartimaeus even knew he would be healed, he cast away his *right to beg.*

This is a crucial lesson that we can all learn from Bartimaeus. I had the *right* to be angry for being molested as a young boy. I had the *right* to be angry at Christians for how they had treated me in the past. I had the *right* to be angry at myself for the choices I made that led to so much hurt in my life. But in order for me to find the healing from

32

my past, I had to cast away my *right* to be angry. Only then could I find healing. I had to forgive.

It's not easy. I literally had to speak out the words:

"I will never be mad at John for molesting me."

"I won't hate Christians anymore for how they treated me in the past."

Most importantly, I had to say, "I will no longer be angry at myself for all the wrong choices I've made." (This included losing complete contact with my firstborn son, Isaiah.)

You have the right to be angry at whatever has happened to you in the past. Maybe it's molestation or a rape. Maybe your parents are divorced or even dead. Maybe someone has stolen something that was important to you. Maybe you've been bullied. No matter what it is that you are ready to face from your past, get a notebook, a blank piece of paper – whatever – and write down what it is.

Whatever it may be, you have the right to be upset and angry. But are you willing to cast away that *right* and run to Jesus for healing?

Believe me when I say that I know it is not easy. But when you cry through it, you will find yourself on the other side. Now you are transparent because you don't care what others think. And I promise, you will feel as though a huge heavy cloak has been lifted off your shoulders.

CHAPTER 4

Every Tree Has a Root

There Is a Reason for It

Ⅰf you have arrived at this chapter not only by reading, but also walking through the processes outlined here, you are well on your way to no longer learning the hard way. You've diagnosed your problems and have begun to find healing from your past. This chapter will continue to help you heal from your past and also to understand the present.

My wife, Annie, and I have a life coach with whom we meet on a regular basis. Let me say that you are never so *fixed* that you don't need fixing. It doesn't matter where we are in life, most of us need help.

Our life coach is Cindy Minard, and she rocks. Annie and I visit with her about anything and everything – our individual issues, our marriage, our kids. I think I've even gotten advice on how to handle our dog before.

Cindy has a saying that has helped guide me in many situations: "Every tree has a root."

We all have a myriad of different trees in our life. I have chopped down some bad ones and grown some good ones, but I still have some nasty looking trees in my orchard. A tree can be most anything – an addiction, a certain way you act or react, a way you treat your spouse or your children, just to name a few.

You may see these problem trees in your life and get frustrated with them – frustrated that you can't get rid of them, even when you've tried hard. But often what we overlook are the *roots.* When I say *roots,* I'm referring to the reasons past events and circumstances cause us to act (or react) a certain way.

The way you act has a reason (or reasons)
behind that action.

There was old guy I used to talk with when I lived on the streets and he put it this way: "Every fact has a reason." Then he would add, "The fact is, you did it. Now what is the reason?"

Either way you say it, it means the same thing. The way you act has a reason (or reasons) behind it. If you are self-medicating with drugs, there is a reason for it. If you are cutting and bringing pain to yourself, there is a reason for it. If you are having anger management problems, there is a reason for it. If you can't be faithful in a relationship, there is a reason for it.

You name the tree that you see in your life – good or bad – and you can be assured there is a root cause or reason behind it.

Fear of Close Relationships

A big problematic *tree* in my life was that I was unable to form a close relationship with anyone. I was always very popular just because I am a fun guy. But I could never go into a deep relationship with anyone. Later on, that included my wife.

I remember sitting and talking with a dear friend (also a counselor and mentor to me), Pastor Lloyd Ziegler. At one point in our conversation, he looked at me in the intense way only Pastor Z can, and he said, "Everyone knows Jeremy Donovan, but no one really *knows who Jeremy Donovan is*."

That hit me like a brick. I realized at that moment that I was unable to become intimate or form close relationships. Once I fully recognized and identified this tree, I began searching for the root.

At first, I simply blamed it on the molestation that happened when I was a kid. However, by that time I had been healed from that root. I had dealt with it and had worked through the pain.

I continued to work on this issue of lack of intimacy that I had in my life, but it was still an unsolved puzzle. I could preach from stage as comfortable and confident as could be, but in a one-on-one situation I was all messed up. I felt awkward and uncomfortable; I got all sweaty and stumbled over my words. I remember thinking that people were looking at me and wondering, *Where did that confident man go who was just up there speaking so boldly from the stage?"*

"There's Your Root"

I became frustrated trying to deal with this root, but that tree of not having intimacy was not leaving my orchard. One day, Annie and I were having a session with Cindy. I'm not sure how it even came up, but I was telling her about my Grandpa and she stopped me and said, "Jeremy, there is your root!"

And it hit me. She was absolutely right.

My grandfather was my best friend in the whole world when I was a kid. I did everything with him. Our last major trip we took together was to Florida to watch the space shuttle launch. Right before I went into my teen years, he got really sick. When he was in the hospital he signed a DNR document (do not resuscitate), so when it came time for the doctors to help him, they could not because he had signed that paper.

I have never been more devastated; I felt like my grandpa had betrayed me by simply giving up and dying. After his funeral, I heard the adults talking about what he had done by signing the document. I remember going up to his room and lying on his bed, punching his pillow in anger. Why would he give up on me? Why would he sign a

DNR? Did he not know how important it was to me that he would see me grow up?

> I felt like my grandpa had betrayed me by simply giving up and dying.

As I sat in that session with my wife, and with Cindy, I began to weep. The root of that problem was finally getting dug up and destroyed. The fact was, I couldn't be intimate with people because I never wanted to go through the pain of them possibly giving up on me like I felt my grandpa had done.

Identify Your Crazy Trees

When you are climbing out of your rut – when you are on the way out of learning the hard way, you need to recognize and identify the crazy trees in your life. Then acknowledge that each one has tenacious roots that want to hang on. You may try to chop down the tree and think that's enough. It's not enough. If you don't go all the way to the roots, that thing will grow back and it will haunt you.

As with my situation, it may not always be what you think. I tried for years to kill my intimacy issues by praying about having been molested as a kid, but nothing worked. It's because I was spraying root killer on the wrong root. It had nothing to do with that.

When Cindy nailed it that it was all connected to the death of my grandpa, I began to find healing. I am now learning how to go deep for the first time. It has helped my marriage, helped my relationship with my children, and with friends. It has also helped me as a pastor.

Matthew 3:10 says, "The ax is set at the root of the trees. So that any tree that isn't producing good fruit is cut down and thrown into the fire." When you keep seeing a tree in your life that is producing bad fruit, you need to find the root of that tree, take an ax and cut that thing out.

When you are dealing with your present problems, it's important to realize that those problems always stem from past hurts and wounds. Going back helps you go forward.

CHAPTER 5

Climbing Out of the Rut

Time for Drastic Changes

If you're serious about no longer doing everything the hard way, then it's time for change. It's time to start climbing out of your rut. Some of you have read up to this point and have walked out some of the principles described here. However, only the people who are dead-serious about changing their life for the better will continue reading to the very end. Because it's at this point that climbing out of the *rut of learning the hard way* gets tough.

It's been said that the definition of insanity is *doing the same thing over and over again, and expecting different results.* If you no longer want to be who you have been in the past, then you cannot keep doing what you have been doing. It is time for some drastic changes.

In order to make those drastic changes, you have to go back to the lesson we talked about in Chapter 3. You have to become like blind Bartimaeus and stop worrying about other people and what they think.

You may need to set up boundaries in your life with some of your friends. In fact, you may have to be willing to allow them to walk away. If you are living in the school of hard knocks, I can pretty much guarantee you that there are friendships in your life that will need to change. There are environments that you will need to avoid like the plague.

> If you're serious about no longer doing everything the hard way, then it's time for change.

Stop a moment and take a long hard look at your entire life and evaluate the triggers that cause you to stumble. It's time to stop allowing them to negatively affect you. It may be time to remove them. You need to be willing to have a *name change.*

Time for a Name Change

In Genesis 17, we find the story of Abram and Sarai. Abram was ninety years old when the Lord appeared to him and said, "I am God Almighty; walk before me faithfully and be blameless. Then I will make my covenant between me and you and will greatly increase your numbers" (Genesis 17:1-2).

Abram had to make the choice to walk faithfully and blamelessly before God. Abram fell to his knees in worship and submission.

God said, "No longer will you be called Abram, your name will be Abraham. For I will make you a father of many nations, I will make you very fruitful."

Later in that same chapter the Lord said to Abraham, "As for Sarai your wife, you are no longer to call her Sarai; her name will be Sarah. I will bless her and will surely give you a son by her. I will bless her so that she will be the mother of nations; kings of peoples will come from her." (Genesis 17:15-16).

At this point, Abraham fell down and started laughing. He laughed and said to God, "Will a son be given to man one hundred years old?" Abraham heard the promise of God, but he was so old that the very thought of having a child made him laugh.

Trust God Anyway

Are you so deep in your rut that a promise of getting out seems to be laughable? Does the idea of your being able to live a good life appear as laughable as this elderly couple having a baby?

In my case, it would have been highly laughable to think I could get out of my rut because it all looked impossible and utterly hopeless. But in spite of everything, I got out! Likewise, it's happened for countless others who have chosen to make the needed changes and to trust God.

There is hope and a promise that God can change your life. You may laugh and not believe, but do as Abraham did and trust God anyway. Try it. After all, what do you have to lose? (Other than your misery and your hopelessness.)

So where does one begin? Remember what God told Abram before he changed his name to Abraham. He said, "You have to walk before me faithful and blameless."

Blameless

Jesus Did This for You

That may sound impossible. How can you become blameless? Becoming blameless in the biblical sense comes about only by understanding the grace God has extended to you. His grace enables you to live holy and blameless before Him. You have to understand what it means to be a child of God.

Jesus came into this earthly realm and died on the cross for your sins. The Bible says, "The wages of sin is death" (Romans 6:23). This means the only way to pay for your sins is by dying. Yeah, I agree that's not something I want to make a payment on. But because of Jesus' sacrifice, you don't have to. You simply have to accept the fact that Jesus did this for you and desire a relationship with Him.

In John 8:58, Jesus said, "Before Abraham was, I am." He was referring to the same Abraham and Sarah described above. The same two people who did eventually see their promise of a child fulfilled – and the Messiah Jesus was in their bloodline.

Now Jesus lived hundreds of years after Abraham, but He could truthfully say, "Before Abraham was, I am." Jesus was not using bad English here, He was stating, "I am God and I am above all time." Jesus was in His eternal existence before Abraham was ever born; Jesus stands outside of time.

Anything that is in the Bible can be proven scientifically, and it is in fact possible to stand outside of time. It has been proven that as you speed up, time slows down. No, it doesn't stop at 88 miles per hour, as in the movie, *Back to the Future*. But at 186,282 miles per second, what they call the speed of light, matter actually propels forward and time stand still. So it *is possible* to be outside of time.

Why is this significant? Because when Jesus said, "Before Abraham was, I am," He was in essence telling us:

"I stand outside of time. Even hundreds of years before my forefather Abraham was born *I am. I always am*. I am that I am."

What does this mean for you?

Jesus Sees You Here

It means that right where you are, as you are reading this book, Jesus sees you here as he is hanging on the cross with all of the pain of the sin that was placed on Him at His crucifixion.

He sees you and right now He stands ready to take all of your dirt and junk that has been keeping you in your rut of learning the hard way. Jesus took it upon Himself when He died for your sins. He has already paid the debt that you owe. When you understand that the price has been paid, and if you accept that gift, it takes you right into the path of being blameless.

Truthfully, if that is all salvation provided, I would be good with that. If it meant only that Christ died for my sins so that I don't have to, I'm good with that. This is totally amazing – there is no greater love than for someone to lay down his life for a friend.

It is so amazing that Jesus paid my debt. I mean, think about it – who does that? It would be like getting into a house that you can't afford – something so many people are struggling with right now – and the bank saying, "Don't worry about it. We'll pay your debt free and clear." Jesus paying our debt for sin is like that, only way *way* better.

Losing your house is one of the worst things that can ever happen to you. It's a nightmare. On the other hand, you will survive. I did lose a house in the past. I'm okay.

But *sin?* Being forgiven for your sins is exponentially greater than being forgiven any monetary debt. When it comes to sin, you have to *die* to pay for that – and yet Jesus took it all for you.

That right there is enough to make you want to give your life to living blameless before him: He paid the price for you to become blameless. But the truth is – good as forgiveness is – salvation is *so much more* than that.

Holy and Righteous

The Bible says that when we accept a relationship with Jesus, not only does He pay the debt for our sins, but "he clothes us in his righteousness" (Isaiah 61:10). Wow, can you grasp what that means? This is huge.

This means that when we make Jesus the Lord of our lives, He not only forgives us of our sins but He clothes us to make us appear to the Father God as holy and righteous as He Himself. That means, according to the Word of God, I am now as righteous as Jesus.

I don't have space in this book to go deep into the message of God's loving grace, as I want to continue giving you tools to get you out of your rut. But I want to encourage you to understand grace in a deeper way than what I just explained to you. To do so, I recommend the book I quoted earlier, *Extraordinary,* by John Bevere. It will change your life and help you understand how God's gift of grace can bring you into an *extraordinary life*. It would be a great companion book to read along with *The Hard Way.*

Access to His Promises

Now that you understand it is possible for you to stand before your Father God totally blameless, you may be ready at this point to accept the gift of salvation. Accepting this gift allows you to enter into a covenant with God that gives you access to all His wonderful promises found in His Word.

I encourage you to say this prayer just as I did all those years ago in my room in *Behavioral Health of the Palm Beaches*:

> *Jesus, I ask you to come into my life and forgive me of all my sins. Come and be Lord of my life. I*

pray as you see me right now, that you take all of my sins as you have paid for them in your death and resurrection.

If you prayed that prayer, and you meant it, that means you are blameless before Him. Your sins are remembered no more. You are positioned before God as good and as holy as Jesus. This has been an amazing and life-changing moment in your life. Be sure to log this important date. Perhaps write it in the front of your Bible, if you have one. Then tell someone – a trusted friend or someone you are sure is a strong Christian.

Faithful

Faithful, Not Perfect

God also told Abram, before He changed his name, that he must be faithful. This is an important part of having a name change and climbing out of your rut. You must be faithful to what God is asking of you. This doesn't mean you must be perfect. I can be faithful to someone as a friend, but still not be the perfect friend. We all mess up. God doesn't want perfection, but he does want a faithful son or daughter who makes wise choices. One who will do what he or she can to live a life that is not destructive.

God isn't a God who sits around thinking up tough rules so that you can have a boring life. This is a common misconception of non-believers. I love what it says in Psalms: "I run in the paths of your commands, because you have set my heart free" (Psalm 119:32). God is your Father. He is everything that a father should be. He doesn't give you guidelines to kill your fun; He gives commands so that you can find freedom and joy like never before.

Commands Not Designed to Ruin Fun

This may be difficult to see from a position deep in the bottom of a rut. We are so used to our junk, we mistakenly believe we must have that *junk* in order to be happy. We are blind to the fact that our junk is a prison. It's keeping us chained to a destructive lifestyle and prevents us from enjoying true freedom.

My two-year-old son is a good example. Cale has a plastic toy lawn mower and loves to *help* me mow the lawn. Summers in Northeast Oklahoma can require you to mow your lawn twice a week sometimes, so this is a time Cale gets to enjoy with me often. Every time we *mow* together, there comes a point where he gets very angry with me. When we get close to our street, I tell him he is going to have to stop following me. This makes him angry. He doesn't understand why he can't walk near the street.

Obviously, I give him this command to keep him from getting hit by a car. My command is not designed to ruin his fun of following me. I love my son dearly and I know what is best for him. I could never live with myself if he were accidentally hit by a car because I failed to keep him away from the street.

Someday when he is older, he will understand my rule that he could not understand as a two-year-old. He will then recognize that that rule gave him the freedom to *live*.

So it is with God. He is our Father and He gives us commands that we may not understand at our current place in life, however, at some point we will. As the scripture states, we will run in the path of that commandment because we realize it gives us freedom. To be faithful you have to understand that God has only the best in mind for you.

Commands Regarding Sexual Relations

One of the most difficult commands for me when I first got saved was in regard to sex. Sexuality was introduced to me at a much too young age, and in a wrong, impure way. All through my teenage years I was having sex. I understood the *no drugs* command because I saw how they nearly ruined my life. But sex? Really, God? I thought God made sex for man to enjoy and so I did. Why wait until marriage? Nevertheless, because I wanted to do right, and wanted to please God, I did everything I could to be faithful to His commands.

It wasn't until after I married my beautiful wife Annie that I realized why God had given us this command. I began to understand the beauty of true and pure sexuality between a husband and wife. I began to understand this command I had been given, and I had to go through many hours of pastoral and regular counseling to heal my mind from the perverted sexuality I had known for many years. I now understand that God's command was to set me free to enjoy a beautiful life with my wife with no worries or hurts from my past.

Here it is in a nutshell – God's command: No sex outside of marriage. This means that once puberty sets in, there is a wait of seven teen years and then a few years of one's twenties. God requires that you keep yourself pure for those few years in order to enjoy forty to sixty (or more) years of amazing sex in a marriage with no pain or hurt from the past.

When you look at it that way, you'll see that God isn't asking you to be faithful to ruin your fun but rather to give you the *most fun.*

Name Change

God told Abram, "Be blameless and faithful to me and I will enter into covenant with you and greatly increase your numbers" (Genesis 17:1-2). Abram fell to his knees and God gave him the new name of Abraham. It can be the same for you. God will change your name if you stand faithful and blameless before Him.

My name at one time was:

- ✓ drug addict
- ✓ street rat
- ✓ jerk
- ✓ bad father
- ✓ liar
- ✓ crazy
- ✓ never going to amount to anything
- ✓ always having to learn the hard way

Then when I became blameless and faithful, God changed my name. I am now:

- ✓ husband
- ✓ father
- ✓ pastor
- ✓ Friend
- ✓ homeowner
- ✓ teacher
- ✓ helper to others who are in one of the ruts I once was in

Are you ready for a name change? Can you be drastic and begin to get out of your rut?

> God will change your name if you stand faithful and blameless before Him.

I talk to so many people that come to me saying they want to change and get out of their rut. So we sit down and evaluate their lives. I will ask them if they are willing to be faithful and blameless. While they may love Jesus, they come up with some excuse as to why they cannot (or will not) change. They leave my office and go right back into their rut.

I usually see them again about the time the boulder smacks them in the face at rock bottom. Boulders to the face and life's bloody noses will often bring people to the point of willingness to make the drastic changes needed. It's my hope and prayer that you will *get it* before that happens to you. The fact is, if you are not willing to make the changes I've talked about in this chapter, you probably will when that boulder hits your face.

Mattie's Story

There is a young lady in our ministry named Mattie. She has grown to be an amazing young woman of God, but she had gone through a lot in her young life. She lost both her parents in her teen years, which led her to a drug addiction and party life in an attempt to self-medicate the hurt that came from losing her parents (along with other pains that came in her life).

She came to our church hurting and quite opposed to anything that was *church related*. However, after a few weeks, we began to see a real change in her. God was softening her and working in her life. She was becoming a real superstar, making all the right decisions to get out of her rut of living the hard way and bringing destruction to her life.

I remember the day when she came to a crossroads of making drastic changes in her life. She called me up and said, "There is a party this weekend for an old friend. I know there is going to be a lot of drinking and I don't think I am strong enough to go through the night."

I asked her why she felt she needed to go. She really had no reason – mostly because of old friends that she hadn't seen in awhile. I began to tell her about how I had to make drastic decisions about changing my life so that I was no longer triggered by those things. I told her that I didn't even go back to Philadelphia until I was way into my recovery process. Even then, I still avoided some of those old *friends*.

I'm glad to say that Mattie made the right choice in the end. She avoided the party.

Friends Who Will Sell You Out

It may sound cruel and heartless to avoid your friends. But the truth is, *friends* in that lifestyle are much different than quality lifelong friends who care about your health and well-being. The people in my old lifestyle simply wanted my friendship so that I could wallow with them in their misery.

You may not believe me but just wait and see. If you choose to stay in your old lifestyle, there will be a point where so-called friends won't need you anymore. Or worse, they may need to sell you out to cover themselves, and they'll do it in a heartbeat.

After the night that I tried to kill myself by taking those pills, after they placed me into the mental ward, my *friends* promised to take care of my stuff for me. After it was apparent that I wasn't coming back anytime soon, it was decided they would hold a garage sale and sell all my stuff so I could have some money through the process.

Garage sale day came and went. I waited and waited for my money. I heard nothing for weeks. Finally, after countless phone calls, I got three hundred dollars in the mail. I had a ton of furniture, a TV that alone was worth more than three hundred dollars, clothes, two cars and much more. My *friends* had pocketed the majority of the money from the sale because they knew there was nothing I could do about it.

Here was yet another point when I had every right to be angry, but I had to give up that right in order to find healing. So I just let it go. However, it taught me that the drastic changes I was making were the right ones.

I promise you this, if any friends leave you because of the boundaries you put in place in order to better yourself and get well, they are not friends at all.

Go Make Your Bed

It is not just friends that you have to be drastic with – it includes all life changes. Remember in Chapter 3 when I described Jarrod's morning routine? "Has anybody told you they loved you today?" he would ask. I would reply, "No." Then he would say, "Well I do and so does Jesus. Now get up and make your bed."

Later I realized he was teaching me something. People who are in a destructive lifestyle (always learning the hard way) usually don't take care of their basic needs. Jarrod was forcing me to make my first drastic change. I had not made my bed in years. It was a huge step in beginning to take care of myself and make drastic changes.

What are some areas in which you can begin to make drastic changes? Start with the small things – as I did in making the bed. Once that is conquered, move on to bigger, drastic changes.

It may mean staying away from certain places that you used to frequent. You may need to set up boundaries regarding acquaintances who are destructive.

Why not start right now – before you go to the next chapter. Put this book down and *go make your bed!*

CHAPTER 6

I've Got Your Back

Medal of Honor

I've spent a lot of time on the streets and in some really shady places. People often ask me why I talk so much about being from Philadelphia. For those of us who lived there, our statement of having survived it is a like wearing a war medal.

People in the armed forces love medals – it's an honor for instance for someone to say, "I was in the Marines and I survived." Now, not by any stretch of the imagination am I comparing myself to the honor due a Marine or any other military person. But at the same time, I have to say, the statement, "I lived in Philly and survived," is a badge that we (those of us who walked that walk) wear proudly.

One of my best friends, Aaron Becker, with whom I share many stories and experiences, was a Marine. In fact,

56

he spent a lot of his service time in the heat of the battle in Iraq. I am very proud of Aaron. This is a man who, even though he fought in a *real* war, will still say with great pride: "I lived in Philly." It is still his medal of honor.

I have earned the "I lived in Philly" medal.

> Those who say, "I don't need anyone," are usually
> the ones who are desperately lonely and need
> people the most.

One of the things that comes out of that lifestyle is a deep understanding of the saying, "I've got your back." It meant you have a buddy who is there to watch over you, and you do the same for your buddy. It's a *brotherhood* thing. Of course, you don't *have* to be from Philly to under-stand this. Even today, living in Tulsa, Oklahoma, I know the importance of someone having my back.

We All Need One Another

I have met many people in my life and sometimes I will hear someone say that they don't need anyone. They are doing fine going it alone. I never believe them. I've learned that those who say, "I don't need anyone," are usually the ones who are desperately lonely and need people the most.

The fact is, we all need other. We can't go it alone. At every point in life you need people.

✓ You need people to teach you skills.

✓ You need people to be customers or clients in whatever trade you may pick.

✓ You need people to take an objective view and give you advice on situations.

✓ You need people for friendships.

✓ You need people of the opposite sex to marry, have children, and create a family.

✓ You need people to do things you cannot do.

Even if you are one of those who have said you don't need anyone, the hard cold truth is, you need people – *the right kind of people* – in your life.

God made no mistakes when He created us. He loves us and He created us in His own image. Think about it – He designed us in such a way that we cannot see the middle of our back without help. No matter where we are standing, we cannot see directly behind us. Hence, each one of us needs someone who will say, "I've got your back."

In the book of Genesis God said, "It is not good for man to be alone" (Genesis 2:18). He designed us to worship Him and bring heaven to earth. He created us so that we would not only need fellowship with Him, our Creator, but fellowship with other humans as well. He created Eve so that she and Adam could inhabit the earth together. God knew we would need others. It was all part of His grand design.

There is great comfort when you hear someone say, "I've got your back," or "I'll stick with you." Especially from close friends who truly stand by you through thick and thin. The comfort is there because we need people.

The Skinny Kid

When I was a teenager, I wasn't the biggest kid around. In fact, I was so skinny it was easy for me to pretend to be sick and pull it off without a hitch.

Once my mother – who could come up with some weird punishments – made me shave my head for something I got caught doing. I was so embarrassed by my bald head that I refused to take my hat off. The problem was my school had a rule – no hats. I wasn't about to take my hat off, so when my teach said, "Jeremy, you need to remove your hat," I sat there for a minute, knowing that I had an embarrassing bald head under my hat. With hardly a second thought, I quickly replied, "I've got cancer." Because I was so skinny, she actually believed me.

Much later, after having friends who actually suffered from cancer, I realized it wasn't cool to fake cancer. But back then, I was a dumb kid who just didn't want people to see my bald head. (Ironically, today I am bald – go figure!)

Someone to Watch My Back

So, with the combination of my small stature and my very smart mouth, I was always in desperate need of someone bigger to watch my back. I had many friends who were big and strong. I can honestly say that I survived my teenage years because of these people. One of these friends, Kevin

Morrison, once stated, "It's not easy being Jeremy's friend, because you are constantly protecting him."

One time when I was a junior in high school, I was smarting off about a kid who was a kid only due to his age. His physique was more like an adult. I'm sure this guy must have been shaving before he was five. His name was Tim and he was about six-foot-four, and over two hundred pounds. Put that up against my five-foot-ten and one hundred fifty pounds, soaking wet self. My odds were not great.

So here I was, the cocky little guy, sauntering around school, mouthing off about how I was going to sneak Tim. *Sneak* was our term for jumping someone. (Now that I'm older I'm sure what *sneak* really meant is *I'm too chicken to stand toe-to-toe with you, so I'm going to get all my big, strong friends to help me jump you*.)

One day during math class, I asked to go to the restroom. I always asked to go to the restroom during math class because I hated math. I would walk the halls for most of the class. I attended one of the largest schools on the east coast, so I could walk for hours. My teacher must have thought I had some serious bowel issues. (I was a good salesman, even at that age.)

One day was different than the others. In my wanderings, I found myself clear across the school from my class. I was all alone and when I turned the corner, there stood Tim. This is when the Bible verse, "It's not good for a man to be alone," took on a whole new meaning.

My first thought was to cut and run before he saw me, but it was too late. Tim called out my name and then walked over and cornered me between some lockers. At that moment I knew I was going to die. He looked down at me and I looked up at him. I thought my neck was going to break; it was like looking up at the Empire State Building.

He said, "I heard you're planning to sneak me."

This is the point in life where I learned to answer a question with a question. I replied, "Now where would you have heard a thing like that, Tim?"

I knew there was no chance I could beat him in a fight. A poodle had a better chance of taking out a pit bull than I did taking Tim down in this hallway. But maybe I could out-smart him. I really wasn't sure of anything at this awkward and terrifying moment. The only thing I was sure of was that I was alone and I really didn't want to be.

Pauly to the Rescue

Just as I was about to pee my pants and beg for mercy, an angel (better known as my friend, Pauly) came on the scene. Pauly was my height, but he was built like a tree trunk. He was a weight lifter and it showed. Pauly was known for being well connected and also had a famous right punch that had knocked many a guy to the floor. One thing was sure – Tim wanted nothing to do with Pauly.

Pauly stepped up and said, "Tim, leave the kid alone." That's all he said. That's all he had to say. I never heard from Tim again.

I could have never faced that giant alone and come out in one piece. All I needed was a friend; someone to help me out.

After Tim walked away, Pauly looked at me and said, "I've got your back, bro."

More beautiful words had never been spoken. I absolutely did not like facing that giant all by myself.

I learned later on in life that this was true for any giant I faced. I couldn't do it alone. My demons, my addictions, my destructive choices – I need people to help me out. These ruts were so deep, it was like looking up at Tim – there was no way I could get out on my own.

You Can't Do This on Your Own

The same is true with your life. You can't do this alone. I don't care who you are, how mentally strong you think you are or how tough you think you are. I promise you, you can't face your giants alone.

On my journey to recovery I found I needed people to

- ✓ give me advice
- ✓ listen to my broken heart
- ✓ pick me up when I was down
- ✓ to show me the tools I needed to face my ruts of addictions and destructive choices

We were born needing to be taught. We all have gifts, but it is other people who teach us the skills in how to master our gifts. When I was born I had an amazing gift of knowing how to eat. But my parents had to teach me how to use my spoon and fork so I could grow the skill of eating like a pro. We need people to show us, to cover our backs and to support us as we face these choices of getting out of a destructive lifestyle.

We all have gifts, but it is other people who teach us
the skills in how to master our gifts.

You may think you have it all handled on your own; you don't need anybody. The fact is, you never know when you will turn a corner and *bam*! there's that giant ready to take you out.

Even today I have giants that I need people to help me with. One of those giants is depression. I can be moving along in life enjoying my roles as a husband, father, pastor, friend and then I come around a corner and *bam,* there's that old depression giant looking to take me out. Depression is something that can take you right back into a destructive lifestyle in a nanosecond.

The typical symptoms that I now recognize are wanting to isolate (back to the "just leave me alone" attitude), and wanting to sleep all day. Sometimes, if it gets bad enough, even though I have been clean for many years, I can start to feel tempted to *pick back up*. (Slang in drug world meaning I wanted go back to the drugs because of the high they offer.) To this day I can have a temptation to pick up. The big difference is that now I know when the giant tries to come back and I quickly turn to those who I know will help me.

I'm sure you've heard the story about David and Goliath. You can read all about it in 1 Samuel 17:1-58. The Bible account tells how David, with God's help, took out his giant. There are times that we will stand in what seems to be the open field of life and face our giants. With God's help, we can. The difference is, sometimes our giants don't die; they just go underground for a while. Some giants we can face for a lifetime. I have learned that the devil will attack me the most when I am alone. This is why depression is so sinister, because you tend to isolate and then in the alone times, the biggest attacks come. This is why I am emphasizing the fact that every one of us need people who will say, "I have your back."

Isolation Can Be Deadly

A young man named Keaton attended the youth group I pastor. He was doing great. He was involved in church, loved God, was popular with the other kids, and even talked about one day becoming a youth pastor. The truth was, he was constantly surrounded by people who loved him and cared deeply about him – people who "watched his back."

Following his high school graduation, however, Keaton began to withdraw. He was seen and heard from less and less. Many of his friends made attempts to reach out to him in love but in vain. Keaton resisted; he isolated.

One morning before dawn, he was driving home from a party, extremely drunk. He wound up driving down the wrong side of the highway and hit a vehicle head on. A couple and their seven-month-old baby were in that vehicle. Only the wife survived. The father and the baby died in that horrible crash.

In one split second of time, Keaton's life was forever altered. Because he withdrew from those who had his back, today he is sitting in a jail cell where I visit him once a week.

It took me ten years to hit rock bottom; it took Keaton only a few months. I can tell you that Keaton has definitely lost the will to learn things the hard way.

Ask God for Trustworthy Friends

I'm so fortunate to have Annie by my side. When she and I were married, I explained – as best I could – the telltale signs to look for when I was heading into depression. On her part, she promised that she would do her best to make me get up and get moving. She has stood by that promise.

I have determined not to allow destructive behavior to affect me anymore. It is so easy to destroy months and months of good simply by allowing one inch of the old destructive lifestyle to slip back in.

I like to compare climbing out of a rut to building a house. It takes months and months to plat out the land, design the house, pour the foundation, build the frame and then finish it out. It's a lot of sweat and toil with many different skilled people coming together to build. It requires months, and in some cases years to build a house. However, it only takes a few moments to tear it down.

The same thing is true for a destructive lifestyle. I have been to the point where I felt like I was almost out of my rut, that I had conquered my giants, only to find that one slight slip, one moment of weakness could tear down so much. Can you relate?

That's the moment you need special people in your life who will say, "I have your back."

You may be reading this and thinking, "I don't have anyone in my life."

I have met many people who don't have supportive family or friends. I have very supportive parents; however when I was going through rehab in Florida, they were over 5,000 miles away in Alaska.

If you don't have anyone you can trust, then you must step out and find friends. Ask God for good, trustworthy friends. Trust Him to lead you in the right direction.

I highly recommend finding a good church in your area where you can find help and find a family. I highly value my present church family.

I have also met great friends in Narcotics Anonymous and through professional counseling. They understood the trials I faced as I climbed out of my deep rut.

If you need help finding connections and people to have your back, I have connections in about every part of the country. My contact information is in this book, so please contact me. I will send you to a place where you can find friends and people who will stand by you and help you. This is so vital to getting out of a rut. You were not designed to be alone.

CHAPTER 7

Transparency Matters

If I Ever Talked, I Was Dead

I can remember drug dealing for some major players on the streets of Philadelphia. I was brought into a lot of areas, houses and places that they did not want authorities to find. I became one of the bigger dealers of ecstasy in the city. I remember going into the warehouse where they were making the pills known as *Omega* on the streets. These were one of the hottest selling ecstasy pills in the city of Philadelphia.

I have to admit, as much as I wanted to be a gangster in the streets and as much as I wanted to be feared by many, when I stood in that warehouse and they were showing me around, I knew that if I ever ratted them out, they would definitely put a hit out on me.

After cutting everything up, the average Omega pill would cost about three dollars to make. The street value on the Omega pill, at the time I was running, was about thirty dollars. I was snorting about two hundred dollars of cocaine a day. The only choice I had to cover my habit was to partner with these people and sell their pills. The secrecy of the operation and the people who owned it was vital. If I ever talked, I was dead. Literally.

An Encouraging Threat

I remember hanging out one night at one of the clubs where I worked. The owners pulled me aside. They felt the need to make crystal clear to me the importance of keeping silence. They threatened me in an encouraging way.

That's right – an *encouraging threat*. This is an old trick of the trade on the streets. They let you know about what's going on and then they encourage you to keep going because *they're on your side.* But don't screw up or tell anyone, because if you do, in a heartbeat, they'll be your worst enemy.

An encouraging threat might go something like this: "I'm proud of you, Jeremy. You've come a long way and you're doing good. But you know you're in deep now. If you ever get caught, screw up or want out, it's not going to be pretty."

It was really an art of the streets. They give you privileged information that must be kept secret, then they had something on you. Now you know too much. Then they threaten you in an *encouraging* way to keep you doing what you're doing. It is such a weird feeling – you fear them and you know you can't say anything, but at the same time you've fooled yourself into believing they really care about you.

I Didn't Want to *Feel* Anymore

After this meeting, I went outside the club and just stood there for a while. Since it was a cold rainy night, I walked into a nearby parking garage to stay dry. I remember thinking that I just didn't want to *feel* anymore. I was trying to figure out this whole mess that I found myself in, but there seemed to be no way out. I knew too much and if I ever tried to get free, they would be after me.

> I remember thinking that I just didn't want
> to *feel* anymore.

That night I had some *Special K* on me. This was a popular drug on the streets at the time. We stole it from vet clinics. It's what they use to tranquilize cats. It's enough to put a cat to sleep, but for a human it just makes you feel *out of it*. People on Special K look pretty much look like a bag of Jell-O and they drool a lot.

I took some Special K to try and self-medicate the problem. "Self-medicate" is the term therapists use to describe the outward and dysfunctional ways that people use to medicate their hurts in life with no professional help. This can be most anything – alcohol, sex, cutting, drugs – you choose your poison.

As I explained in an earlier chapter I was what people called a *garbage head,* meaning I would self-medicate with just about anything that was put in front of me. About the only thing I never did was shoot up. Mainly because I have, even to this day, a phobia about needles.

That night as I sat in that garage the weight of everything was bearing down on me: I knew too much and I couldn't tell anyone. They had me with that old trick on the street of letting me in on just enough – enough for them to have something on me, so then they could *own* me with their threatening encouragement. In order to block out the nightmare, I chose to self-medicate. I needed something to put me out of my misery.

In the Dog House

Cocaine wakes you up. It's what they call an upper because it pumps you up. Since I needed a downer, I went for the Special K. It took only a few minutes before I went totally out. I don't remember another thing about that entire night. However, I'll never forget the next morning when I woke up.

When I awoke I was aware of being curled up in a small, dark space. I was shaking from a mixture of the cold, rainy weather and from coming down off my high. A beam of light shone through a half circle door cut in the front of the space I was in. I crawled out through that hole and found myself in a backyard, surrounded by a privacy fence that was typical in the backyards of Philadelphia.

I will never know what happened that night, but somehow I had made it from Old City to North Philly. Due to the cold rain, I guess I discovered what seemed like a logical place for an addict to spend the night – *in a dog house in the back yard in one of the worst parts of the city.*

My hidden life began to drive me crazy. It's what the streets wanted, for you to know their secrets so they can hold you captive; it's what the streets demanded. They own you.

The Original Gangster

This plan is not original with these bad guys on the streets. It comes from the original gangster – the one we know as Satan. Satan went against authority (God) and was removed from heaven, and thus he began his miserable life.

This is something you will learn – sooner or later – if you continue in a destructive lifestyle. The people on the streets don't really want to be your friend. What they really want is company in their misery. They just don't want to be alone.

This was Satan's position as well. He needed someone to share his misery. So he went to the Garden where God's beautiful creation, Adam and Eve, lived and there he tempted them. They sinned by disobeying God. And what did they do next? They hid. That's right. Because now they had *something to hide.*

This street idea of giving you privileged information so they have something on you is straight from the dude himself – the devil. This strategy is the one that all the other bad guys live by. If you have something to hide, then you're trapped. Because if anyone knew, it could ruin you. What you don't realize is that secret (or secrets) is ruining you.

All of the secrets that you are forced to carry take so much of your life that sleeping in a dog house, surrounded by dog filth, in the freezing rain seems acceptable.

If you have nothing to hide then you have nothing to lose. The devil knows this, so he wants you to have things to hide. Then he can give you the encouraging threat: "Just keep doing what you're doing, but don't ever let anyone find out. It can ruin you or kill you."

So you continue on, hiding what you don't want others to know, and you think that by hiding it, you are saving your life. But in all reality it's killing you and it makes sleeping in a dog house acceptable.

My Friend, Mary

I'll never forget a revelation moment I had a few years ago. It's one of those moments where someone else might say, "Well duh," but for me it was huge.

I love learning from people who are older; who have lived life. I was sitting in a retirement center visiting my friend, Mary. I used to visit her every week when I was in Master's Commission at the Christian Bible College I attended in Florida. (More about Master's Commission and how I got there later in the chapter.)

Visiting Mary and ministering to her were part of the requirements of the school. Strangely enough, as it turned out, Mary ministered to me much more than I ever ministered to her.

Another of the requirements at Master's Commission was to dedicate our entire first year to God. This included no dating – or anything close to it. This was not easy for me at all. Much as I hate to admit it, I was already breaking the rules. I had started dating a girl at the coffee shop. It seemed like a win-win setup because I liked her and she knew how to make good coffee.

For some reason, I found myself telling Mary about my coffee shop girlfriend. I suppose it was because I felt I could trust her.

After she heard my confession, she said, "I thought you weren't supposed to have a lady friend in your first year of school."

I smiled and said, "You're right. That's why I'm keeping it a secret."

She looked at me in the most motherly way possible and in her soft southern drawl said, "Jeremy, if you have to hide something, I can guarantee you should not be doing it. *You don't want the devil to have anything on you, do you*?"

Transparency Matters

Her words hit the mark. As she said that about not wanting the devil to have anything on me, my mind flew back to that night in the club. I remember how I hated knowing those *secrets.* Because I had something to hide, they had something over on me. That's how they held me captive and that's why they could give me those encouraging threats.

At that moment, I saw it clearly: If I have to hide something then the devil has it over on me. Not only should I not be doing it, but the devil then has something on me and I'm in his grip. I'm held captive.

This is why it's *so* very important that you have transparency in your life. When people used to try to threaten us on the streets, if we weren't scared of them we'd simply say, "You don't have nothing on me."

I never really understood that until this revelation hit me. *Your life can't be threatened if they don't have anything on you.*

It is so important that you understand that *transparency matters*. In the last chapter, I emphasized the importance of having friends in your life who will help you face your giants. If you are not transparent with them, however, their friendship will not be helpful to you. And if you cannot trust them enough to be transparent, perhaps you need a new friend, one you *can* trust.

Find a Few Trusted Friends

I'm not suggesting that you be transparent with the whole world. Find a few friends, a strong support system. These should be friends who will lift you up in your battle to get out of your rut. They should face your giants with you.

Be open and honest with these trusted friends about what you are dealing with. If it isn't hidden, you can look at the devil and say, "You don't have anything on me." His threats no longer matter.

The Bible says, there is nothing hidden that will not be revealed (Matthew 10:26). I don't believe this means that things will be revealed in order to embarrass you, but simply that God knows the importance of the devil not having anything on you. He doesn't want sleeping in a dog house to become acceptable to you.

I have had so many things in my life I felt I needed to hide. When exposed, each one was painful to me, but afterward, I felt free and clean. Some things I have confided to my closest friends – those I trust and those who help me fight giants.

Other times, I knew God wanted me to share something for my testimony. As I did, freedom came to me. When that happened, I could look at the devil and say, "You have nothing on me."

Have no fear now. Dog houses are no longer acceptable. Be transparent. Don't fall into that old street game of allowing the enemy to hold anything over your head.

Find those friends who can help you face giants; those friends you can go to and share your struggles and mistakes. Learn to be transparent with them first. Your transparency will bring the freedom you need to get out of the rut. No longer will you have to learn the hard way.

One Dark Secret

After I became a pastor, I gave my testimony at many different places. My goal then, as it is now, is always to help people get out of their ruts. This is what I've devoted my whole life to.

I've told my story in front of thousands in huge churches. I've told my story in school assemblies and in small class-rooms. I've told my story at concerts and on the streets to three or four gang members and addicts – whoever would listen. I've told my story to people in one-on-one settings. If a door opened for me to tell my story, I took it.

But... but! In all those times that I've told my story there was one part that I could never bring myself to tell. I could tell about being molested as a young kid, I could tell about the drugs, the girls, and the mental wards. I could tell how Jesus my Lord saved me from all of that.

The enemy had me convinced that people could and would overlook all of the above, but no one would ever accept me if they knew I had a son when I was only nine-teen and that, because I was considered to be an unfit father, I had lost custody and eventually lost contact with that child.

The enemy had me convinced that people would accept me as a pastor if they knew I'd been set free from drugs, and set free from the wounds of being sexually abused. After all, I'd heard other pastors share similar testimonies. But no one would ever accept me as a pastor if they knew I wasn't allowed to see my son because I messed up so bad that his mother didn't want to see me, even after I began doing better.

This lie of the enemy meant that he had something on me and, therefore, held me captive. For years I told no one except those who were the very closest to me. I could never talk publicly about my son – I just couldn't risk it.

Breaking Free

Finally, I came to the day when I knew I had to be free from the enemy's *encouraging threats.* (*Yeah, Jeremy, you're doing great now, but just you wait. If they ever find this out about you, it's over for you as a pastor.*)

In great fear and trembling, I went to my pastors and told them that I was thinking about addressing the entire congregation about my son, Isaiah. At this time, Pastor Glenn was preaching a sermon series titles, "Breaking Free," and I knew that I wanted to break free from this wretched embarrassment of failing as a teen father. I wanted to break free so I could talk about my son, openly pray and then birth fresh hope that one day I might have him back in my life.

Pastor Glenn supported me fully. He saw that it was a great *fit* for the series.

That sermon changed my life forever and allowed me to at last be totally and completely transparent in my ministry.

It was May 15, 2011. I'll never forget sitting on that front row in our first service, shaking and thinking, "What if they all reject me?" I looked over at Annie, and said, "Baby, is this the right thing to do?"

"Yes," she reassured me. "You love your son. Now let's let everyone who loves you know about him."

I'm usually a fairly confident speaker – and especially in my home church. That morning I shook with fear. I stood there and told my story to my church family. For the first time in all those years, I explained all about my son, publicly.

As I got to the end, I was shaking and crying. I walked off the stage and paused for a moment to collect myself. As I looked up there was a line of my church family coming toward me, all crying, waiting to give me hugs, pats on the back and words of encouragement.

Open Doors

Through the following weeks, I received a whole slew of messages on FaceBook and through emails, thanking me for opening up. Many were specific in explaining exactly why and how my story helped them.

I've heard Pastor Glenn say it repeatedly:

> **"What you think disqualifies you for ministry**
> **is what actually qualifies you."**

From that moment I was set free from the fear. That decision has helped me stand even stronger in my ministry. What the enemy said would destroy me has worked to quite the opposite effect. It has opened doors for me to help people in a larger dimension than ever before. I still walk with a limp from those things – especially wanting to reconnect with my son – but now my heart is free and my mind is clear. It feels so good. The enemy has nothing on me.

"What you think disqualifies you for ministry is what
actually qualifies you."

I believe there are people – even pastors – who are in ruts and they think, "I should be farther along than this." They're holding onto things in their lives that will come back and tear them apart.

Without transparency there can never be true freedom. You must not keep things in. This doesn't have to be some public thing where you stand up like I did, and tell the world what you have done. But to the people you trust – those who are there to help you face the giants that come; the ones willing to get in your dirt and help dig you out of your rut – these are the friends with whom you *must be one hundred percent transparent*.

Have at least one pastor and friend you can trust. If you don't have one, get hold of me and I will help you. You need this covering to get out of your rut. If you don't, I promise one day you will be saying, "I'm still stuck; I should be farther along than this."

CHAPTER 8

Do They Think
You're Crazy Yet?

You Have to Get a Little Crazy

After ninety days in rehab, I lived in a halfway house until I went to Master's Commission. During that time, even though I'd been clean for months (in the mental ward and then in rehab), I found I still craved drugs. I still craved and wanted to go pick up.

It's puzzling how even when you see that life is getting better and is finally worth something, your flesh will beg you to go back to learning the hard way. That old nature constantly begs you to jump right back into that rut.

I'm glad to say that even with the cravings, I didn't pick up. I believe part of it may be due to being strong minded. When you are coming out of your rut, you have to be steadfast. More than that, I believe the main reason

I stayed clean was because I was *crazy* enough to change my environment.

You may be wondering why that would be crazy. Well, trust me, if you want to get out of the destructive lifestyle of learning the hard way, you have to be a little crazy.

I often talk to people who, after hearing my story, will say: "Jeremy, I love your story and where God has brought you. I've given my life to God too, but I just seem to keep messing up."

That when I tell them: "I can help you, but you're going to have to get a little crazy with your choices."

Let me explain this more clearly. If you want to get out of your destructive lifestyle of learning the hard way, you will look absolutely crazy to the people *who are still in it*. This can be really hard. Why? Because, as a general rule, a person coming out of a rut has very close friends with whom they relate. And also, as a general rule, those close friends are also in the same type of rut (or an even deeper one).

So here you are trying to get clean, trying to improve your life, and those old friend are saying things like:

"You're crazy."

"Why are you being so stupid about this?"

"You're letting all of your friends down."

"Why would you do this to all your friends?"

Their words will hurt when you hear them; you'll find that you want to make them happy. You want to stay in the good graces of those old friends. We all have this little person in us that wants to please people.

I've Been There

This is why so many people fall into the trap of peer pressure. It's not so much that we want to go back to that destructive way of living. We just don't want people to think that we are not cool or that we're letting them down. So we go back into our toxic lifestyle. I know this for a fact – I've been there.

I remember sitting out in the parking lot of Club Egypt – a famous nightclub in Philadelphia back when I was around. I was hanging with a close friend; someone I was dealing with on the streets.

By this time, I had already had my brain aneurysm and been in and out of mental institutions. This was getting close to the very night when I tried to end it all. I was tired of the way I was living and wanted to stop. This so-called friend didn't know my desperation. As we sat there in his car, he pulled out my weakness – a bag of cocaine. I stared at the bag and said to him, "Man, I'm not really into this today."

He replied, "Come on, bro, just have some fun with me."

So I did.

As I look back, I realize that at that moment I wasn't snorting to get high; I was snorting because I didn't want to let my friend down. (Ironic, but so true.)

This happens a lot when you're trying to make a life change. You always have those people who are going to make you feel bad and call you crazy for what you're doing. At that point you *have to be willing to be seen as crazy*. You have to be willing to lose friends, to change your environment, to change the way you do things. As I said earlier, you have to be drastic in order to get out of your rut.

I was snorting because I didn't want to let my friend down. Ironic, but so true.

As I said previously, the definition of insanity is doing the same thing and yet expecting different results. You can't keep doing the same things. You can't keep living the same way in the same place and expect to get out of your rut. Your environment must change.

I knew I had to change my environment. I had to do drastic things to the point where people in my old lifestyle thought I was crazy. I finally reached the point where I didn't care what people thought. I didn't care if I let people down who wanted me to party with them. I became more and more determined not to go back to that old lifestyle.

Change Things Up

I love the story of Gideon's army in the Bible (Judges 6-8). People must have thought Gideon was nuts. As he was getting ready to go into battle, in obedience to God, he cut the number of his fighting men by more than half. And even before he did that, he was already vastly outnumbered. God told him that he would not win the battle by doing things the way they'd always been done: "You'll have to change things up to win this battle."

It is the same way with your rut. You can't win your battle by doing things the way you've always done them. You will have to change things up.

You will hear me say this over and over again, but it's crucial to your getting free from the rut – you must take drastic steps and stop worrying about what other people think.

I had to do drastic things to the point where people in my old lifestyle thought I was crazy.

When I got into Master's Commission, I had given up all drugs and drinking. I still dealt with cravings, but because I changed my environment so drastically, I had no idea where to find the things I craved. But here was the stickler – the thing I struggled with the most was smoking. I had been smoking two to three packs a day for over five years and it wasn't easy to quit.

Some of you reading this may be thinking, "Is smoking a sin?" I may make some pastors upset by saying this, but no, I don't think smoking is a sin. I love what my dad says: "Smoking won't send you to hell, but it could get you to heaven a lot faster."

I must clarify now – while I don't think smoking is a sin, I do know it's a stupid and highly addictive habit. I think smoking is not only unwise, but I believe it can curtail anything you try to do in life. People don't seem to hold as much respect for a person who smokes. In my case, I knew I wanted to be a youth pastor; therefore, I knew I had to quit smoking. It was *not easy*. I can, without reservation, say that smoking was one of the hardest things I had to come off of. Tobacco is so addictive that even to this day, when I get upset or stressed, I will still crave a cigarette.

Cold Turkey

I knew for me to ever become a pastor, I would *have* to quit. So I got crazy – I quit cold turkey. So when anyone tells me they can't quit, I know they just don't want to quit. I smoked two packs a day for years and I quit cold turkey.

This is how I did it. I never went into places that sold cigarettes because I knew I'd buy a pack. That's right. I'm not trying to say I'm this great tough guy who could just quit cold turkey. I had to *change my environment.* I had to get crazy enough not to go anywhere near cigarettes.

When I went to the convenience store to gas up the car, I never went inside to pay – I paid from the pump. I knew the cigarettes were right behind the cashier where I would be paying. I also knew I wouldn't be strong enough, *so I never went in.*

There were a couple of times when I was thirsty and needed to get something to drink. But still, I would *not* go in. I stood outside and offered to buy someone's drink if they would go into the store and get one for them and one for me.

Did they think I was crazy? Probably. Did I care? No. I knew what was required and I was willing to pay the price.

How willing are you to get out of your life of learning the hard way? Are you willing to get crazy and change your environment?

Accountability Software

I have a friend who struggled deeply with porn. It was a bondage that kept him up into the late hours of night. Just as I did with cigarettes, he quit porn cold turkey. It was time to get crazy. He moved his computer out of his bedroom and into the living room where the kids could see. (He was helped greatly by the site, www.xxxchurch.com, which has proven very effective in helping men and women beat porn addiction.)

My friend accessed the free accountability software from that site. The software is designed to compile every site he visits, then email those sites to the people he selects. He chose: 1) his wife, 2) his pastor, and 3) his mother. This meant he was deadly serious about breaking that bondage, because now he was accountable to these three special people in his life. When the temptation came to go browsing like before, knowing that special people in his life would see his actions stifled it.

My friend completely changed his environment to get out of the rut he was in. Today he can stand up and say he is completely free from addiction to porn. He's still climbing out of his rut and going through the healing process with his wife and family, but he is free, clean and happy.

Some of you are reading this and thinking, "I really don't want to put my computer in the living room and I definitely don't want people seeing the websites I'm visiting."

Well, just as Mary, my friend told me, "If you have to hide something, you probably shouldn't be doing it."

If you're not willing to be called crazy, you may never get out of your rut. I don't want you to look back someday and *wish* you'd followed through and used the tools that I'm introducing in this book.

I truly want you to be free!

CHAPTER 9

Emotions vs. Emotional

Fly Off the Handle

When I was coming out of my rut and my addictions, I was extremely emotional. Many things were surfacing, such as past hurts and mistakes. I was starting a whole new life. I could no longer be a part of the life I'd known before. These changes were not easy and I would fly off the handle in a split second.

I remember one Sunday, I was on the rehab bus that took us to church. We called it the "Druggie Buggy." I'm not kidding. Well, it was pretty funny. We were shuttled in this huge blue bus that had the words *Behavioral Health of the Palm Beaches* painted on the side. Every Sunday, all of us *patients* would climb out of the "Druggie Buggy" and head inside. We were quite a sight.

On this particular day, I was laughing the whole way there, acting silly and having a blast. I got to church and cried through the whole service. (The preaching wasn't even that good – I was just crying.)

After church, we got back on the bus and were headed back to the rehab center when I totally lost it on a guy. I was literally screaming at him and cussing him out. He had done nothing wrong – it was all *me*.

I got off the bus, went back to my room and sat there thinking. I started laughing again, realizing just how emotional I was. In one short expanse of time, I went from happy to sad to mad and back to happy again.

Let's face it, we're all emotional, but even more so when we're going through extreme changes. I can promise you – the changes you are going through to get out of your rut of a destructive lifestyle will make you more emotional than you've been in a very long time.

Emotions are Not Your Enemy

Emotions are not your enemy. Emotions are actually from God. He Himself has emotions. If you study the life of Jesus, you'll see that while He lived as a man on earth, He experienced all the emotions that we experience.

Emotions are not wrong; however, allowing your emotions to control your decisions will cause you to make decisions based on feelings rather than based on consideration of the consequences the decisions may bring.

God has emotions but He is not *emotional*. His emotions never control or persuade His decisions. It's important for you to *understand* your emotions and to not always trust them.

"You Look Just Like My Son"

One time I was in the shopping mall right after I had shaved my head. (I'll admit it wasn't a style choice. I'm balding and shaving it looks better than a comb over.) As I walked through the mall a lady came up to me. She had tears in her eyes when she looked at me. She said, "You look just like my son."

Being the personality I am, I replied, "He must be good looking."

She smiled and said, "Yes, he was. I just got word he lost his life in the war."

I felt horrible and began to apologize – the pastor in me came out. I truly hurt for her.

She stopped me in the middle of my apology and said, "I have desperately wished I could have just one more day with him. I think this may be it. Would you do me the favor of just spending the day with me at the mall?"

I don't know about you, but there was no way I was telling that lady no. I had a long day of shopping planned anyway, so I said, "Sure I was just heading to my next store."

As we began to shop, I picked up a shirt and she would pick up the shirt too. I found one I liked and decided to buy it. She picked up one just like it.

She said, "Son, do you like that shirt?"

There was a pause because I didn't know what to say.

She said with tears in her eyes, "Oh I'm so sorry. Is it okay if I call you son? I really just want this to be like my last day with my son."

Of course I had no other reply except, "Of course, Mom. I love when you call me 'son.'"

As we shopped, everything I purchased, she did the same. I finally asked her, "Are you going to buy all the same things I buy?"

She looked at me again with tears in her eyes and said, "Yes, I... I want to have all the things my son would have gotten on our last day together."

===

God has emotions but He is not *emotional*.

===

I really almost lost it there. It became a very emotional day, but I knew I had to make this the best day for my *Mom of the day*.

Finally I said, "Mom, I think I need to get going."

She said, "Yes, me too." So we went to the register. As we stood in line she said, "Son, this has been a wonderful day, but it took way longer than I thought. Could I check out my items first?"

I said, "Of course, Mom. I'm just glad we got to spend the day together."

The cashier rang her up. Then the lady I'd been calling Mom all day looked at me and said, "Son, thank you for this memorable day."

"You're welcome. I would have had it no other way."

With that she turned and walked out the store.

When the cashier finished ringing up my purchases she said, "That'll be $745.00." I almost fell over. I said, "There's no way – how can it be that much?"

"Well sir, when I was ringing up your mom's purchases, she said that her wonderful son would be paying for hers today."

I couldn't believe it. I had been hustled by an old lady! I dropped everything and ran out the door. When I saw her, I yelled out, "Mom!" (It was the only name I knew her by.) When she saw me, she began running to her car. I sped up to try to catch her. She got to her car and jumped in, but just as she was about to slam her door, I dove and grabbed her leg. I started pulling on her leg hard to pull her back out of the car.

I was pulling on her leg about as hard as I am pulling on yours right now.

That's right – I'm pulling your leg. Sorry to have done that, but I wanted to use this as an example. This is the *fiction part* of this book. It was one hundred percent made up. Now why would I do such a thing? Why would I put fiction in a book like this?

Your Emotions Cannot be Trusted

I wanted to demonstrate to you that your emotions cannot be trusted. Some of you, as you read the story, may have gotten fairly emotional. But that's all it was – just a story.

Emotions can be tricky. As I said earlier, God designed our emotions and they're an important part of who we are. But if you allow emotions to rule, you'll make unwise decisions. We can't always trust our emotions because all of us can get emotional – even over things like the story I just told.

We've all watched movies and TV shows that made us laugh, cry, get scared or angry. We get emotional over things that aren't even real. But it's not just the media that does this to us. It's all of life.

So many times I've gotten angry at someone over something I thought they did – or said – only to find out it wasn't really true. I felt so bad for getting angry at someone for something they didn't do!

There are times in my life when I've stressed over things simply because I didn't know all of the facts. I allowed emotions to rule and I made bad decisions. I have come to learn the only reason I'm ever stressed or worried is because I don't know all the facts. As soon as I understand all the facts, even if they are not all good facts, I no longer worry.

When you're climbing out of your rut, you'll come to many moments that will bring emotions. Some are real and some are fake, but no matter how real or fake they are, emotions are always there. They are there, rising up inside of you: happiness, sadness, anger, worry, bitterness, jealousy, frustration – the whole gamut.

Logic Rarely Comes Through Your Emotions

If you want to get out of your rut, it's time to stop making decisions based totally on your emotions. Instead, you will take things that come your way, think about them and carefully evaluate them. Logic rarely comes through your emotions. To get out of your rut, you need to learn to understand this.

> If you want to get out of your rut, it's time to stop making decisions based totally on your emotions.

The difference between *having emotions* and *being emotional* is this: An emotional person gets upset and resorts to self-medicating – whatever form that might take. Having emotions means that person understands the emotions and works through them to make a logical decision.

When I was deep in my rut and I got upset, my reaction to that emotion was to get high or drunk. Now when I get upset, the emotions still come up inside of me. However, now I stop and think. I use wisdom to make clear and logical decisions. The choices I made to use drugs and alcohol never addressed the real problems. In fact, they introduced even more wild and unruly emotions.

Before when I was angry, I allowed it to rule me. I would fly off the handle, punch walls and say things I would later regret. Today when I get angry, I first stop to acknowledge the anger is there and that I can't think clearly. I then remove myself from whatever situation is making me angry. I calm down, assess the situation and make decisions logically.

I also often call my friends who help me face my giants. I'm transparent with them and ask them their advice in the situation. Sometimes when you know you are emotional, the best thing to do is get advice from someone who is totally removed from the situation, who has no emotions involved.

I do this even with things that don't seem *bad*. For instance, if I'm about to make a big purchase and I feel myself getting all happy that I am about to get something new and cool, I call someone who has no emotional attachment to the purchase or investment. That person will usually ask me questions that I might never have thought of. Looking at things from another perspective calms my emotions and helps give me wisdom to make the right decision.

If you can become aware of your emotions, learn how to control them and learn how to make decisions that are not based on emotions, you'll find yourself climbing out of the rut much faster.

The next time you want to pick up, drink, or do whatever it may be in your destructive lifestyle, take a moment to identify the emotions that triggered you. Call those close friends and ask them to talk you through your emotions to help you to figure out why you want to go back. If you can do this, you'll greatly increase your success in getting out of the rut.

CHAPTER 10

12 Days Is Longer Than 12 Years

The First Time I Tried Beer

When you're coming out of a rut and choosing to live life differently, whatever you were doing to self-medicate will be a hard habit to break. They say it only takes thirty days to create a habit but it can take years to break. I believe part of that is true. I also believe when you are hurting and need something to take the pain away, you can create a habit in an instant if you like whatever you try.

I'll never forget the first time I tried beer. I was fourteen years old and went to a keg party. I started to drink and man, it felt so good. At fourteen, I had no idea how much was too much and I almost drank myself to death at that party, but I remember how great it felt when it was happening.

The next morning wasn't as fun. No one told me that if I drank too much, I could get sick. I had to learn that on my own. I never went to the doctor, but I'm sure I had alcohol poisoning. I was sick for three days after that party.

Instantly Created a Habit

Now you'd think after all that pain and agony of throwing up for three days straight, I'd be done with alcohol forever. It was just the opposite – I instantly created a habit. This is what an addict – or someone who is self-medicating – does.

I am sure if you have ever struggled with a destructive lifestyle behavior you know what I'm talking about. The first time you had a drink or smoked a joint. The first time you stuck a needle in your arm. The first time you overate. The first time you starved yourself. The first time you cut yourself. Whatever it was, and even if it hurt, you seemed to feel better for a few minutes.

The problem with these fixes is they are extremely short-lived. Nothing I did ever lasted more than twenty-four hours. After that, I needed to do it again to get that same feeling. This is how you graduate from the *temptation to try something* into *bondage*.

No Lasting Fix

Do you know what I mean by bondage? It's when you know what you're doing is going to hurt you. You know the feeling will not last more than a few hours. But in your desperation, you're willing to do it for those few fleeting moments of feeling better.

This is one of the major problems of the rut. Everything in it that you choose to make you feel better has no lasting fix. Within a few hours you need it again. It brings you up and then takes you right back down. What a cycle. Go out to the clubs and get drunk. Do some drugs. Have sex if you can find someone. Then you're home alone, sick, feeling guilty, and terrified that you might have caught something.

Instead of picking yourself up to find help, you get depressed. In your mind, the only remedy is to go and do the same thing over and over again.

I remember one night I was at a club I frequented. I drank the same beer, stood in the same corner, and danced with the same girls. I remember standing there wondering, "Is this all there is – this same old stuff that I'm doing over and over again?"

The days will never tell you what the years will.

This destructive lifestyle brings you into the habit of existing from day to day. The devil actual likes to see you in this predicament because he knows that anything of quality in a person's life always takes more than a day to accomplish. Anything worth having takes time and effort.

The days will never tell you what the years will.

So if the enemy can get you to the place of the *quick fix,* and if he can convince you that this is the only way to survive, then he's happy, because you're now in *bondage.* Bondage is not easy to get out of; it takes time.

Now the Rut Is Deeper

As I worked to get out of my rut, I came to realize that *twelve days is way longer than twelve years.* Several times, I came to the point where I thought, "I want to get out of this life. I need to quit this." I would even reach the point where I threw my drugs out and tried to get away from my friends.

That would last maybe a few days and then my mind went crazy. I experienced uncontrollable urges to pick back up. I was desperate to go do something to give me that quick fix of making it all feel better.

This is how I became a garbage head. Usually, on the second or third day of trying to quit, I would go nuts and search for anything I could drink, snort, or take. I simply couldn't handle it and I fell right back into my rut. Only now that rut would be deeper than ever.

I know that many of you reading this can relate to what I am saying. You want to stop in the worst way. Your family and friends scream at you, "Why don't you just stop?"

All the time you are thinking: "I want to more than you know."

But every time you reach that point where you can almost believe you have the courage – you really have what it takes – to get better and to get free, you make it two or three days and then fall right back into it.

I want to encourage you that this is *normal* for one trapped in addiction. This is exactly what you've trained your body and mind for. This is what the devil wants you to think – that you absolutely cannot make it more than a day. Listen to me when I say this: *Twelve days is way longer than twelve years.*

Celebrate Milestones

All of the anonymous clubs (Alcoholics Anonymous and others) give out medallions or tokens to celebrate milestones along the way. It begins with a 30-day token, a 60-day token, and then a 90-day token. Once a person reaches the 90 day sobriety milestone, the next one commemorates the six month achievement. From there, the celebrations are on a yearly basis.

Any addict who has ever gone through one of the Twelve-Step programs will tell you that the *30-day token is the most difficult*. That special medallion is the one that most addicts cherish and keep forever.

Those first thirty days are definitely the most difficult – and of those, the first *twelve to fifteen days are even more difficult*.

The reason behind this is exactly what I explained earlier. You've trained your mind and body for the quick fix.

When your mind and body feel down, you've taught them how to get a quick, happy feeling right away.

So during the first thirty days, you have to do exactly what all the experts say – you must create a new habit to replace the old. I've been clean for almost twelve years now. I cannot tell you that that feeling to have a quick fix doesn't ever come back, because it does.

Many times stress will come at me and, in a flash, the thought crosses my mind of how nice it would be to have a drink or do a line. Yep. It's true. Even as a pastor, these thoughts can come. But I will quickly add that after twelve years, I am stronger than ever before. The battle has gotten easier with each passing year.

The first twelve days felt like hell.

The first twelve days seemed *way longer then the twelve years*. The first twelve days felt like hell. A year was tough. Twelve years – not so bad. Why am I telling you this? I want you to see the road out of your rut. The devil doesn't want you to see this. When he sees you trying to get out of your bondage, he'll throw things in your way to trip you up. Hard times will come. People will be in your face offering all that tempts you.

The only way to win this part of the battle is to grasp the truth: Your freedom and happiness are found in the *years,* not the days (or even the hours).

Yes, it seems like a giant you can't beat; like bondage that will never let you go free. But that's not true. Your success in getting out of the rut will be seen in the years.

I can tell you that today I'm happier, more contented, and have more inner peace than I've ever had in my life. I would never give up what I now have for a quick fix. Because the happiness I've found in the years lasts for years; it's not just for a few hours like my old *quick fixes*.

CHAPTER 11

Detox

No Longer Powerless

Sometimes I like to compare a *rut* (destructive life-style) to having a bout with the flu. You know you're hurting, you know you aren't making good choices, but you just don't know how to fix it. This fact used to drive me crazy because I knew what I was doing was hurting me (and everyone around me), but I felt powerless to stop. The steps I have given you in this book will change all of that for you. *You are no longer powerless.*

One aspect of the flu that I do know how to handle is *rest.* When I get sick, all I want to do is go home, lie down and sleep. This is actually a good thing. It's what we're supposed to do. When we sleep, our bodies actually go into a healing process.

Annie accuses me of getting the flu way too often. The truth is, I'm worn out and need rest. (Look everyone! I'm putting this in writing – *my wife is usually right*.)

Every person needs to set aside time for quiet and for rest in order to heal and recover when we're sick. The same is true for you when you're coming out of your rut. It is crucial that you take time to rest in order to heal yourself. This is so vital to getting better. In the drug world this is known as *detox* time. You have to rest. You have to sleep. And for addicts who have been spiraling downward – you have to *eat*.

... a person can be in a destructive lifestyle and
not be on any drugs.

Most people, when they hear the word "detox," think only of drugs. But a person can be in a destructive lifestyle and not be on any drugs. Detox simply means to cleanse. Sometimes it feels selfish to simply stop and rest; or to reach out and ask people to help you. However, it's vital that you do so.

It's not only your body that needs rest, it's your mind and emotions as well. It's difficult at first to comprehend how much garbage is being carried around in the mind. But as I stated earlier in the book, this destructive lifestyle didn't simply drop on you by accident. A mind cleansing will take place as you stop and rest.

If you're going to make it out of your rut, it requires a lot of effort. This means that sometimes you will need to get away, clear your mind, and allow your emotions to settle. I love to take moments in my day and just stop and clear my mind.

Mother Teresa, the woman who chose to live among the poorest of the poor in Calcutta, India, aiding them with food, schools and medical care, was once asked a candid question in an interview.

"Mother Theresa, when you pray, what do you say to God?"

She replied, "A lot of times I don't say anything."

The one who was conducting the interview was stumped. He then asked, "Well if you don't say anything, what does God say to you?"

Her answer? "A lot of times, He doesn't say anything either."

This statement speaks volumes to all of us. (Or it should.) What a precious gift just to sit in the presence of God the Father and feel His love.

Mistakes Catching Up With Me

I remember going through some crazy times coming out of my rut. Unexpected things would pop up that made me realize that getting out of the rut was going to be a lot harder than I first thought. Mistakes I made in the past were now catching up with me, such as money I owed for the legal process; emotions I had tamped down inside me because I had suppressed them for years with all the drugs.

One day, I was sitting there in the rehab center thinking things were getting a little bit easier. I'd cleared through a few obstacles and felt I was gaining ground. At that moment, I got a phone call from my mom in Alaska. She'd just received in the mail an envelope stuffed full of old traffic tickets of mine from New York City. (My mail had all been forwarded to my parents' house after I went into rehab.)

I had totally removed myself from the rest of the world. This is a common process for people in deep ruts. I didn't open my mail or answer phone calls for months. So when my parents started getting my mail, they were shocked by all the bills that were months behind.

The saddest part about these tickets from New York is that they were from a part of the city I couldn't even remember being in. I spent a lot of time in Manhattan, but had no idea why I would be getting tickets from Harlem. It frustrated me; it was a huge bump in the road that I didn't need at the moment. After that, more and more bills that I'd been ignoring kept coming in.

It was at that point that I almost lost it. Back to the old whines:

"Why is this happening to me? I'm doing better. I'm trying and trying, but it just doesn't get easier."

Ever been there? This is the point where many people give up on the process of getting out of the rut, when it gets so hard and even looks impossible. I've heard so many people say the almost identical phrase: "This is just too hard. I give up."

And if they give in at that moment, it's back to the rut.

My message to you is, when you get to this point of climbing out of the rut (notice I said *when,* not *if* – it's pretty much a given that you'll hit this wall), I want to encourage you to STOP and detox. It's time to clean out all the stuff that's swirling around in your head. Get away; get quiet and pray.

When you get this upset, when you are experiencing this much turmoil, when the attack is the strongest, it's almost impossible to think straight. It's almost impossible to make wise decision. Remember this:

Never make permanent decisions because you are temporarily upset.

Decisions made when you are upset are decisions you will usually regret – *especially if those decisions involve quitting on your improvement process.*

I Found the Strength to Continue

When those things began to go wrong in my life, it would have been so easy to cash it all in, to say: "I quit. This is just too hard." There were moments when I really thought I would quit, but then I would stop and think back. I looked at where I'd been and how far I'd come. I knew I didn't want to throw it all away, no matter how painful the present seemed to be. As I reflected on these things, I would always find the strength to continue.

If you stop and reflect back to your life in the rut, yes, there may be a few fun memories, but if you're entirely honest – that life sucks. There's no reason to want to go back there.

When you are coming out of your rut, there will be times when everything seems to go wrong. When it seems there may not be any way out. It gets so overwhelming, all you can think of is how easy it would be to just slip back into that old lifestyle – where everything was familiar. But I want to encourage you to stop worrying about all those things and focus on the one thing that matters, and that is, Jesus.

In Luke, chapter 10 of the Bible, Jesus comes to the home of two sisters named Mary and Martha. He comes to have dinner with them. Martha gets so excited that Jesus is coming, she wants to make sure her house is in order and that He feels welcome. I can understand how she feels. I mean, if I knew Jesus – in the flesh – was coming to my house, I'd want everything to be perfect. I'd even take time to clean my garage just in case he wanted a tour. I can't imagine the excitement I would have if Jesus came to eat at my house.

When Jesus arrived, Martha was running around getting the food ready and making sure Jesus was comfortable. As she's doing all this, she notices something that frustrates her: her sister, Mary, is sitting quietly at Jesus' feet. I can relate to that frustration.

I Relate

When I was a teenager, my sister, Sarah, was seven years younger than I was, and my brother Josh was four-teen years younger than I was. (Yes, weird, but we are all exactly seven years apart.) There were times I had to do chores and my siblings, who my mom thought were too young to help, would sit around and smile at me.

I remember how frustrated I was when my mom asked me to help my sister hang up her clothes. Sarah sat on her bed and smiled at me while I hung up her clothes. It made me fume.

One day, I'd had enough and yelled to my mom, "Do you realize she's old enough to hang up her own clothes and she's sitting here laughing at me while I have to do her work?"

Mom couldn't believe Sarah would be so sneaky. She came into the room and asked Sarah to show her if she could reach the clothes in the closest. Sarah said, "No I can't," and then stood three feet away from the closet so she couldn't reach. That's right, she had to stand three feet away to "not be able to reach."

Needless to say, I won that battle and that was the last time I had to hang up her clothes. My sister is an amazing person and I could never have stayed mad at her. (I think she learned most of those tricks from me anyway.)

But as you can see, I understand how Martha felt. She was doing all the work and Mary was just sitting there at Jesus' feet, listening.

Like me, Martha hit her breaking point. She'd had enough. Martha went straight to Jesus and said, "Jesus, don't you see my sister just sitting there at your feet while I'm slaving away doing all the work?"

Jesus looked at Martha and said, "Martha, you are worried about many things, but Mary is focused on the one thing that truly matters."

What a powerful statement! While Martha fussed and worried, Mary was totally focused on Jesus and His words – on what He said mattered most. She wanted to soak in everything He had to say. Deep in that spirit part of her being, she realized that she had a moment to be in the presence of the Savior of the World, Jesus the Christ. She sat in His presence and found peace; therefore, she wasn't worried about all those other things.

Detoxing in God's Presence

This is how I found peace coming out of the rut. I would *detox* myself from all of those things I was worried about. The rehab center where I lived was located right on the beach. (I know – tough, right?)

One day, down on the beach I actually *found* a discarded inflatable beach mattress. It became mine. I would lie on that inflatable mattress and float out in the canal between Singer Island and the Florida mainland. I'd float right out in the middle, with boats passing all around me. I'm sure they wondered, "Who is this nut on an inflatable mattress in the middle of the canal?"

I couldn't hear their thoughts, nor did I even care. In my own way, in my own style, I was *detoxing*. I would lie out there and clear all the junk out of my head. I would get away and sit at the feet of Jesus. Many times, I sat in silence like Mother Teresa talked about.

It's Crucial to Stop and Rest

I can't tell you this strongly enough – it's crucial that you stop and rest and get in His presence. Especially when everything seems to be coming at you – when everything looks like it's falling apart – stop; detox; rest; get into His presence and hear His words. Most important of all, stay still until you fully experience His presence in your life.

I can't tell you this strongly enough – it's crucial that you stop and rest and get in His presence.

It's amazing how you can sit in His presence and not say a thing while He doesn't either. But when Father God holds you in His presence, I promise you, it brings a peace that passes all understanding. You will find peace and begin to make the right choices.

I repeat: You can't always trust your emotions. *Don't make permanent decisions over temporary emotions.*

Martha was worried about many things and it brought her frustration. Mary was focused on one thing – Jesus – and it brought her peace and a history-making moment.

The same can be true for you. You may not have a beautiful canal in Florida. (I don't either anymore. There are no beaches in Oklahoma.) But I encourage you to find your own place where you can get away and rid your mind of everything that's coming at you.

This way you can find peace in Jesus, and you will get direction from Him on how to make non-emotional (wise) decisions. Those kinds of decisions will help you stay out of your rut.

One thing I was good at while in my rut was not facing the consequences of my actions. It was much easier to stay in my delusion and pretend problems didn't exist. That's why I never read my mail. I didn't want to face the hole I'd put myself in.

I've since learned that it's way better to face giants head on. I've learned that once I detox, I can face my giants with more inner strength.

I began to think of all the hurdles that might come my way as I climbed out of my rut. While it wasn't possible to think of all of them, by allowing myself to rationally consider them, the more immune I became to those emotional, blindside punches. You can do the same thing.

Please, take time to get quiet, to get away. Be like Mary – focus on the one thing that matters. That one thing is *Jesus*.

CHAPTER 12

Risk for the Good

Incredible Risk Takers

A few years ago, a study was conducted in which fifty people over the age of ninety were asked a challenging question. (I learned about this study from an amazing communicator, Dr. Anthony Campolo. I used to love to hear him preach even when I was running from God.)

In the study, they asked these individuals this question: "If you had the chance to live life all over again, what would you do differently?" When the many answers were distilled down, three distinct answers emerged from the study. The interviewees said if they had it to do all over again:

- ✓ "I would risk more."
- ✓ "I would reflect more."
- ✓ "I would do more that lives on after I am gone."

Those are powerful answers. However, I have to say that most people who are still in a rut and living a destructive lifestyle don't have to be told to take a risk. Most of them are incredible risk takers. Most addicts are the type of people who never do anything halfway. If they're going to do something, it's going to be foot to the floor and no stopping.

Most addicts are the type of people who never
do anything halfway.

In some respects, this is a good quality to have. Too many people live boring lives. I'm talking about the average American. Statistics show that eighty percent of the people in America, by age thirty, hate what they do for a living. The risk-taking addicts look at them and laugh. (I used to laugh at them too.)

The point here is that while risk-taking is not a bad quality, it's just that addicts risk in the *wrong way*. Trust me, addicts look around them and they aren't sure they want to come out of their rut and live a boring, mundane lifestyle.

Begin to *Risk Right*

I'm here to tell you that there are different kinds of risks. I want to encourage you, as you come out your rut, to learn how to take risks and do it the right way. In other words, you will begin to *risk right*.

I took so many risks while I was in the rut and bent on learning everything the hard way. (There are too many stories to share here.) In a way, it was all very exciting, and truthfully, I loved that part of my life. I didn't like the pain that the lifestyle brought. I didn't like the rock-bottom, bloody-face moments. But I loved taking risks and I didn't want that to stop. So what I had to do was learn how to *risk right.*

My first big right risk moment came when I telephoned a Bible college from the rehab center. Sounds nuts, right? I called a college known as Master's Commission. Master's Commission is a discipleship program and Bible college started by an amazing man and one of my pastors, Lloyd Ziegler.

I told them I was in rehab and that I had been clean for ninety days. I also let them know that I had no money, very few clothes, no car and *a really bad smoking habit*. I also quickly added that I knew I had a call on my life to help people. I knew I wanted to live for God and be a pastor.

That was my pitch to Master's Commission.

Now most people in their right mind would probably not take the risk of calling a Bible college and telling them they had been clean for ninety whole days and couldn't pay for college. Nor would they likely top it off by asking the college to accept them and their smoking habit. But Fort Myers Master's Commission heard my story and accepted me anyway.

I remember picking up the phone that day and thinking, "The worst they can say is no." That's where I was – just willing to take risks and see where God would take me. For the first time in my life, I started to take right risks.

Where is that Place?

My roommate in Master's Commission was Gerry (pronounced *Gary*) Blaksley. Today Gerry is one of my greatest friends. He looks out for me and helps keep me out of the rut.

After we were done with our studies at Master's Commission, Gerry asked me what I was going to do next. I said, "I guess I'll head back to Philly."

Of course after all the time we'd spent together, he knew my sordid story. He said, "You can't do that, Jeremy. Why don't you just come to Oklahoma with me?"

I loved taking risks and I didn't want that to stop – what I had to do was learn how to *risk right.*

Now I didn't even know people lived in Oklahoma. I don't think I ever said the word *Oklahoma* until I met Gerry. As a kid, I remembered watching that horrible scene of the Oklahoma City Bombing and wondering, "Where is that place?"

I don't mean any offense to Oklahoma, because it's been the best place I've ever lived and it would take a lot for me to ever move from here. But when Gerry asked me to come with him, I was scared. It was a place I didn't know. I knew one person in Oklahoma and that was Gerry.

But I felt like it was a better choice than going back to the environment that got me in so much trouble.

I'll never forget arriving in Owasso, Oklahoma, for the very first time. It was the first time that it hit me: "The world isn't overpopulated after all. There's so much open space here – it's awesome."

Amazing Changes in One Short Year

Gerry's family members are business people. They have three sons: Gerry, Travis and Dustin. Gerry's parents, Alan and Stacey Blaksley, took me in and made me a part of the family.

They live in a very nice house on a ton of land with all kinds of stuff like in-ground swimming pools, and a private plane. I remember that very first night at their house. It was during family dinner (yes, it still happens in America) that I sat there and reflected back. One short year before, I was locked up in a mental ward. Now I was sitting in a huge home, eating great food with an awesome family.

I was quickly learning the right risks have great rewards.

Alan put me to work at one of his companies, his ranch. Now let's talk about taking risks. The only cows I'd ever seen in my life were when our school took us on field trips to see them. Nevertheless, these ranch people threw me on a horse and said, "Go round up them cows."

I never liked to say I didn't know how to do anything, so I was very clear that I *knew how to ride a horse*. That horse took off running and I almost died. I had absolutely no idea how to ride a horse. The horse reached the middle of the pasture and decided to stop and eat grass. I couldn't get him to move again and proceeded to have a fifteen-minute talk with him about how stupid he was making me look, and to please start walking again.

Oklahoma became the best right risk I ever took in my life. I met my beautiful and amazing wife, Annie, in Oklahoma. Today I serve as a pastor only a few short miles from the ranch where I first started working. The Blaksleys are like a second family to me. Gerry, Travis and Dustin are like my brothers, and Alan and Stacey are spiritual parents to me. I love them all and am thankful and honored that they call me their *adopted son*.

I could have gotten scared about going somewhere I had never been – a place where I knew only one person. There are those who would have looked at that situation and said, "That's way too scary. It's a whole lot easier to just go back to where I'm comfortable." But I took the right risks. I did things in a situation where I had no idea what I was doing, but in doing so I learned so much.

Today I can ride a horse; I can help birth a baby calf; I cannot break a tractor, in fact, I can actually even drive one. I learned a great deal about running a business and so much more. But above all – the biggest thing I learned was to risk right.

It is SO Worth It

Many of you reading this book are willing to risk for drugs or something else that put you in your rut (or that will cause you to hit the boulder at the bottom). But for some reason, when it comes to risking right, it stops you dead in your tracks.

The fact is, when you take risks that will better your life, it is SO worth it. I'm not saying that all of my risks have worked out. The truth is, some have failed miserably. Many jobs I applied for in ministry were rejected. I have taken risks to reach out to different influential people, and while some have become great friends, others shut the door. I'm sure they told their secretaries to never take a call from *that guy* ever again.

But I don't regret those failures (if you can call them failures). That thought doesn't even come up as I look back. When I look back, what I regret are the risks I should have taken and didn't; things I knew would have made my life better and brought some of my dreams to fruition even faster. That's when I wish I had risked more. Those moments in my life when my spirit was stirred to do something great and I calmed it down by telling myself they could never work? I regret those.

That's why I am telling you that, on your way out of the rut, it's okay to risk right. Do those things that you know God has put in your heart to do. You risked for the bad things that you self-medicated with and now I'm asking you to risk for the good. Risk for the dreams God placed in your heart.

I want to encourage you as you come out of your rut. Don't lose that risk- taker part of who you are. Don't lose your passion to go all out.

Just learn to risk right.

If I can do it, you can do it!

CHAPTER 13

Helping Others Helps You

Vital to Your Success

A huge part of getting out of your rut is to help others. It's a proven fact that helping other people is vital to success. In fact, history has proven that success will rarely come if there is *no contribution to others*. All of us, as human beings, have a deep longing to leave a legacy. We want to be remembered in a favorable light. The biggest and best way to do that is to help others.

Helping others, however, is about way more than leaving a legacy. When you reach out to help others – it actually helps *you*. Why is that so?

First of all, by helping others, we learn from them and learn about ourselves as well. I know in my own life, when I'm counseling others I'm giving myself counsel at the same time.

Secondly, helping others gives you a sense of responsibility. It's much harder to mess up when you know others are looking to you and counting on you.

At this point, you're probably thinking, "Who am I going to help? I'm a mess."

I promise you, there's *always* someone to help. And, believe it or not, you *are qualified* to do it.

You are Called

I like what my pastor, Glenn Shaffer, says when someone tells him they are too messed up to help anyone: "What you think *disqualifies* you for ministry is often the very thing that *qualifies* you."

But now, I've gone from talking about helping people to talking about *ministry.* What's going on here? You're probably thinking, "I'm sure not called into the ministry."

... history has proven that success will rarely come if there is *no contribution to others*.

Let me clarify something. If you believe that Jesus is the Son of God, and if you've asked Him into your heart and made Him Lord of your life, then you are *called into ministry*.

Another profound thing that Pastor Glenn says is, "Every member of the Body of Christ is a minister." (I wish all of you could move to Owasso, Oklahoma, and learn under

Pastor Glenn. I know you can't but I promise you, these words are correct.)

Whatever you're supposed to do in life, that is your *ministry;* and the very thing that you think *disqualifies* you, actually qualifies you. Even when you don't think you're ready.

Let me give you a profound, life-altering example of what happened to me in this area.

Deep in My Rut

My 22nd birthday was not a good one. It had only been a year since I suffered from the brain aneurysm. Life wasn't good at all. I was so deep into my destructive lifestyle, so deep into my rut, there appeared to be no way I would ever get out.

I got very drunk that day and continued on my daily drug habit. I was in my apartment most of the day, sitting on my bare mattress on the floor in the corner. The dishes in the sink had mold all over them, but I didn't want to disturb them because if I did, it set off the horrible smell of rotting food.

My apartment was a mess; my life was a mess. I hadn't seen the ones I loved in months because I had hurt most of them to the point where they finally gave up on me. I knew I needed to get some sleep because I had to go to work the next day. At that point, I was working as a truck driver during the day and in the nightclubs at night.

I had to be at work early, but I couldn't sleep because my mind was tortured with the reality of what my life had become. I felt so depressed and desperately wanted to end it all. There seemed to be no point in living.

The Fateful Day

The next morning – the day after my 22nd birthday – I was in my truck in New Jersey. The radio was on and at that moment, the radio DJ, Howard Stern, said words I will never forget: "*A small plane has crashed into the World Trade Center.*"

I was shocked. Being in New Jersey, close to Newark, I wasn't far from being able to see the Manhattan sky-line. I drove closer and was quickly able to see what was happening. It was pretty obvious that it had been no *small* plane.

Yes, my birthday is on September 10! The day before the fateful day that changed America – and the world – forever. I'm sure everyone reading this book knows the rest of the horrific story of what happened that day.

After the Trade Center buildings collapsed, it dawned on me that there were hurting people in the middle of all that destruction. In a split second of time, the mess in my life no longer mattered.

Leadership Skills Rose to the Surface

The leadership and organizational skills that lay dor-mant inside of me rose quickly to the surface. I started making phone calls and put together a team, along with a truckload of donations. I put together an interesting team of people: a youth pastor, three of his church leaders, two business men, and Hans who ran the streets with me and was like my little brother.

Miraculously, we got into the city before they closed it down and made our way to The Bowery Mission. The Bowery Mission is a homeless mission near Bowery and Canal Streets just outside of lower Manhattan – the exact place where everything was closed down within hours. In short order, The Bowery Mission was transformed into a supply center to deliver supplies to people in the city who needed them.

I stayed at the mission with a few others and began to help. We hopped into trucks and ambulances and headed to Ground Zero where we delivered supplies to help in the rescue operations. Later, it was no longer a rescue operation, but became a clean-up operation.

It was strange, but the drugs I thought I couldn't live a day without, I now lived for weeks without. I was so busy helping others I never gave a thought to self-medicating.

I had the privilege of meeting the police chaplain, Pastor Richard (Rick) Del Rio, founder of Abounding Grace Ministries and Abounding Grace Church in New York City. Pastor Del Rio is famous for his tattoos, his leather jacket, and his Harley. He's known as *the pastor on a Harley-Davidson*. I had the privilege of riding with him and assisting him as we prayed for people around Ground Zero.

Special Moments

There were many special moments I experienced while staying at the Bowery in the weeks and months after 9/11.

A very stirring event happened at about two in the morning a few days after the attack.

There were a few dozen firefighters, policemen, and paramedics, mixed in among the homeless guys who lived at the mission, along with me and my friends. We were all exhausted from working for days – with no breaks – searching for survivors. I remember that we were just standing around talking when all of a sudden, one of the homeless guys started singing, "*Amazing Grace, how sweet the sound, that saved a wretch like me...* "

Everyone stopped talking. His voice started off a little weak and wavery, but then grew stronger. Then one person's voice joined with his, then another and another and another. Soon we were all singing until the high ceiling of the chapel at The Bowery Mission was filled with the beautiful refrain of that old hymn. Believe me, that's a moment that will stay locked in my memory forever.

Another heart-wrenching memory was the day we'd been asked to take food and water to the *identification building*. This was the building where they put watches, rings, clothes, wallets, purses, or any personal items (no matter how small) that had been found at Ground Zero.

It's difficult to describe the scene. People waited in line to try to identify some little bit of something that had belonged to their lost loved one. That line extended for blocks – it appeared endless. This is the area you may have seen on the news because this is where people started hanging pictures of their loved ones in hopes that someone might recognize them and maybe – just maybe – they could be found.

Along with my two friends, Hans Hufstetler and Cal Seidel, I began handing out food and water to the people. We got about halfway down the first block and there stood a little four-year-old boy. He stood close to the curb and his eyes connected with mine. I will never ever forget the look on his face. You could see in his eyes that he had been crying, but seemed all cried out. What was left was a look of fear and pain like I'd never seen before.

This little boy was holding a sign with a picture on it of a business man who looked to be in his mid-thirties. The sign said simply, "Have you seen my dad?"

I went over to him, knelt down and said, "Do you need something to eat or drink?" He looked back at me with those pain-filled eyes and muttered, "No thank you."

We continued to work our way down the line, but then we stopped. We needed a break. We crossed the street and sat on the curb and just cried together. I will never forget that boy; he changed my life forever. Every time my life gets hard, I think back to the pain that came to him on that beautiful morning of September 11, 2001 – the day that turned his young life into a nightmare.

I Made a Difference

Why am I telling you all of this? Because I feel that I made a big difference by staying and helping at The Bowery Mission. I feel that God used me in those months after

9/11. But you'll remember that I said the very day before – my birthday – I was drunk and high and hating my life.

Whether or not I was qualified to help at the mission never came up! No one was taking applications!

That's why I can say to you, it's never too early to be of help to someone. It will change your life when you do. There's no greater feeling, no drug that can give you a high that even comes close to the exhilaration you feel when you help someone in need.

I knew then that I was *capable* of helping people and doing things that left a legacy.

I continued doing this sort of thing all through the time of getting out of my rut. You see, after I got done helping with the 9/11 relief efforts, I didn't *go good* from there. No! Remember I'm the one who has to do everything the hard way.

I Knew I Was Capable

I went right back into my rut; doing my same old thing. But I have to say, I *knew something had changed in me from that experience*. Even though I still couldn't see the way out of my rut, from that point I knew I wanted to do something great that would change history. Because I knew then that I was *capable* of helping people and doing things that left a legacy.

Just like after my aneurysm, as much as I wanted to be better, I simply didn't have the tools. I didn't know how to help myself. So I returned to the only thing I knew.

I hope that by this point in the book you feel you now have the needed tools to get out and stay out of your rut.

Helping people during 9/11 helped me. Now 9/11 is over, and I pray nothing like that ever happens again in our nation, but there are still places where you can help; there are hurting people all around you.

Leading a Bible Study

When I was in rehab, I knew I wanted to make a difference. So with the help of my amazing counselor, Leslie Knowles, I started a Bible study for the other patients. It started with two or three of us every morning, but soon grew into about ten.

I loved teaching people about the Bible. I didn't know that much about it myself at that point, but I knew more than most of the people that came out every morning to hear what I had to say. This experience taught me how important helping others was to my recovery and to getting out of the rut I was in.

All of a sudden I had ten people who looked to me as a spiritual leader. Yeah, me. Just a few months off cocaine, and I was teaching them. Leslie Knowles believed in me so much she started telling churches they should hire me as their youth pastor. With all of these people looking to me and believing in me, it increased my determination to stay clean. I didn't want to let them down. I now had a *reason,* a fresh *motivation* to stay out of the rut for good.

Go find someone to help because I promise you – it will help you.

CHAPTER 14

It's About Generations

See Beyond You

The Bible makes it very clear that *generations* are important to God. The New Testament starts by explaining the genealogy of Jesus. It was important to prove that the prophesies from the Old Testament were true – that Jesus did come from the seed of King David. He had to be from a royal family in order to be the King of Kings.

In this chapter I want to help you see beyond you – beyond your life – to the generations that will come after you. This will help you grasp the reality that what you do today will affect generations to come.

There are many examples in the Bible where one individual's choice affected the lives of hundreds of generations. One of the more profound examples is the story of Abraham. Yes, this is the same that guy I talked about earlier who was a *risk-taker*. I do admire his fearless faith to follow God (Romans 4:16-19).

But even when you have faith like that of Abraham, you may sometimes feel that God is taking way too long to fulfill His promises – so you step in and make unwise choices.

Affecting Generations

I've said this before, and I'll say it again: *your choices matter*. It's a given that your choices affect your life, but have you ever thought that your present choices will one day affect the generations who come after you? It's true. Abraham learned this lesson. And guess what – he learned it *the hard way.*

> ... have you ever thought that your present choices will one day affect the generations who come after you?

As I said earlier, Abraham was a risk-taker and he risked right. He had faith in God; once he'd heard from God, no one could stop him. God promised Abraham and his wife, Sarah, a child. They weren't young when they got this promise. They were rounding up to one hundred years old.

Even before they got this promise they did exactly what God told them to. They left their home country and headed out for a land hundreds of miles away – a land that was unfamiliar and unknown to them. Wow, what a risk-taker.

The important thing to understand here is that risks can be good if you *risk right*.

Imagine getting a promise from God and then moving out and taking a gigantic step of faith, and then nothing happens. You did everything God asked you to do, and then you sit back and wait, but the promise does not come. God promised Abraham and Sarah a child, but no child came.

I understand that situation. I've had dreams in my heart of things I wanted to do, but then I'd get impatient, thinking God was asleep or wimping out on me, so I got in a hurry and ended up making bad choices.

Let's put Abraham's position into perspective. He was seventy-five when God first told him he would be a *father of nations*. When he turned ninety, the promise was given to him once again. Now he's nearing one hundred years old, and guess what? Still no child!

I am sure the closer Abraham got to the "big 100" mark, he was beginning to think, "I'm no spring chicken; something better happen, real quick."

Bad Choices

So, like a lot of us do, Abraham and Sarah began to try to think of something *they* could do to bring the promise about. (This is so not true by the way. If God promised it, then it *will* happen.)

Evidently they did not realize that their choices not only affected them, but greatly affected the generations to come. By this time, Sarah was convinced she would never be able to have the promised baby, so she suggested to Abraham that he go and lie with her maidservant, Hagar. Abraham thought about it. It made sense to him, so he agreed with Sarah's idea. At that point, he took matters into his own hands. The child born to Hagar was named Ishmael.

Even though Abraham and Sarah made a bad choice, and it seemed all was messed up, God still fulfilled his promise. What a sign of God's amazing grace in our lives.

Sarah did become pregnant and she had the son God promised. His name was Isaac, which means *laughter.* God does have a sense of humor.

Just as God promised, Abraham had many sons. Out of Abraham and Isaac came the Jewish race. But due to Abraham's bad choice, he also birthed the Arab race through Ishmael. Today both of these two races are still at war.

Abraham had no idea that his decision would create a war between his sons and the generations that came after them. I think if he could have seen the generations to come, he may have had more patience to trust in God's promise.

What I pray for you is that you see the generations after you. Your legacy does not lie in the memory of your present life, but in the people you raise up for the generations to come. It lies within your family, your children and those people I told you who are there to help in your recovery process.

Many people fail at life because they lack a vision for the generations to come. I have seen people so intent on being *remembered* that they become selfish and hurt others in their quest to become *famous*. What they don't realize is by wounding those people around them, they are losing – or distorting – their legacy.

Not Just About Me

I started coming out of my rut in a more powerful way when I realized it wasn't just about me. Of course I knew I had hurt the people in my life through my addictions, and through my penchant for doing things the hard way. However, it took a while for me to understand that my choices would affect the generations coming after me. A choice I make today could be as impactful as Abraham's choice was. It could change the way of life for my children and their children.

I believe my parents have created an awesome legacy for their children. They are still happily married. They instilled in their children a love for God that all of us have tried to run from, but cannot due to the undeniable truth that they taught us. We have family traditions and memories that I want to pass on to my children and grandchildren.

Our choices do matter to the generations to come. If I were to go back to that destructive lifestyle of my past, there's a chance my children would learn those habits as well.

Close the Doors to Destruction

Stop a moment and think about the habits and behavior patterns you may already be struggling with. I am sure if you look back at your family you will see things there that you struggle with today. It could be alcoholism, drug addiction, divorce, anger – so many things that can go from generation to generation that are a part of a destructive lifestyle.

The generations do matter and I want to encourage you to close the doors in your life to adverse things that have been passed on to you from the generations before you. Then close the doors that you may have opened to the new destructive things. Think of the choices you have made that you definitely would not want your children to do, and it's definitely not something that you want as part of your legacy.

Now you can't just say *I close those doors for my children and my legacy* and it suddenly happens. That would be like me sitting in my living room and yelling at my front door to close. I have to get up and do it myself or it will never close.

Second Corinthians 5:17 says, "Therefore, if anyone is in Christ, he is a new creation; the old has gone, the new has come!" I love the exclamation point at the end of that verse. It's like the Apostle Paul – the author of 2 Corinthians who found so much freedom from his former life – was shouting this statement out with joy.

Once you accept Jesus into your heart, you are a new creation! The old is gone! The new has come! Through Christ you will discover your new creation. Understand that it's about generations and close those doors.

I want so much for your legacy to be that of a person who lives a whole and healthy life. When your grandchildren become adults they can say, "I learned thus and so from my parents," or, "I learned thus and so from my grandparents," or, "I heard that my great-grandfather (or great-grandmother) was one who cared enough to change the entire direction of our family and gave us the legacy we have today."

I'm asking you to look into the future and see one hundred years from now.

Just as it was with Abraham, your choices aren't just about you, they are about future generations. As was stated earlier, your legacy isn't in the memory of your past life; your legacy is in the people you raise up for the generations to come and the choices you make that impact them.

Even if you don't have children, you still affect the legacy of your family. My uncles and aunts had a definite impact on my life as a child. No matter where you are – even if you think you are all alone – your choices affect the generations.

When I realized how vital this was, it made me come out of my rut quickly and shut the doors that could destroy my legacy. I thought about my children and the people who look up to me and I knew I had to shut those doors. I did it even for those not related to me because my legacy lives on in whoever I am helping. (This goes back to Chapter 13, *Helping Others Helps You.*)

I thought of my son, Isaiah, whom I've not seen in many years. I know that if we are ever reconnected, I want to leave a legacy for him that he can be proud of. I daily pray that I will see him soon. However, even if I never see him on this earth, I know there's more to this life than the natural realm. In the spiritual realm, it's important I make the right choices and leave the right legacy for my son, whom I may never see here on earth.

I Finished Well

What is your legacy right now? Think about the rut and begin to make the right choices to get out, because it's not just about you. If you need to seek forgiveness, then do so. And even if the other person will not forgive you, you know you've done your part. Don't let it be on you. Leave a legacy that says, "I went through my junk; but I finished well."

Leave a legacy that says, "I went through my junk; but I finished well."

Mark and Joseph

One of my favorite stories is about two high school students. I'll call them Mark and Joseph – definitely not their real names.

Joseph was the guy the other kids in school called "the geeky guy." He was socially awkward and constantly picked on. He was a very smart kid who tried to concentrate on his school work, but he was constantly distracted by the cruelty of other kids. They never took the time to find out what an amazing person Joseph really was. All they knew was what they saw – they knew he didn't act cool, he didn't dress cool, and didn't have the coolest hair. They pegged him as an easy target.

Joseph hated to go to school. Sometimes he was punched in the face or got his head shoved into a toilet for no reason. While he was sitting at lunch, kids would walk by and push his lunch into his lap. Every day it was something and it was getting to be too much for him to bear.

One day Joseph stood in the hallway at his locker. He had an armload of books and papers that he was trying to shove into his locker. While he was getting them all in, some bullies came by, knocked all the books and papers out of his arms and began to kick them all over the hallway.

Joseph knelt down and began to cry as he picked up the mess. He hated for them to see him cry, because he knew that would let them know they were getting to him. His classmates just stood in the hallway laughing as Joseph was on his knees crying and picking up the mess they had made.

At that moment, Mark came walking around the corner. Mark had a different experience in school than Joseph. He was the star quarterback and head of the Fellowship of Christian Athletes (FCA). Every girl in the school wanted to date Mark and every guy wanted to be his friend. Mark came around the corner and saw Joseph on his knees, picking up his books and papers, crying while other people just stood and laughed.

Mark had seen Joseph before and had seen the kids picking on him, but never like this. This was too much. Mark knelt down and started to help Joseph pick up his stuff. All of the sudden the laughing stopped. Some of the student who had been laughing got down and started helping too. They definitely didn't want to be on Mark's bad side.

Mark helped Joseph pick up all of his books. As they stood up, Joseph wiped away the tears from his eyes and with a sniff said, "Thank you for noticing me."

Mark thought that was an interesting response and thought, "This kid must feel like no one ever notices him. That's not right." So he said to Joseph, "What're you doing tonight?"

Joseph replied, "What I do every night – I'm going home."

"Well, since that's all you're doing, how about if you come to my house and hang out."

Joseph thought for a minute and then said in a scared voice, "Sh… sure, I'll come over."

A Lot in Common

That night the two young men found out they had a lot in common. Joseph told stories of things he had been through and so did Mark. It was the start of two young men who became best friends. In the next few days, word got around that Joseph and Mark were now friends. Joseph was never picked on in school again; no one was going to pick on Mark's best friend.

Mark and Joseph stayed best of friends throughout high school. Helping Joseph in turn helped Mark, because as it turned out, Joseph was incredibly smart. Since he was no longer being picked on, he had plenty of time to study and reached the top in his classes. Joseph helped Mark study and enabled him to keep his grades above average.

Upon graduation, Joseph was the valedictorian of his class. On graduation night, he got up to make his speech. He started out by thanking those who had "helped me get where I am today." Then he continued:

> *But I need to start by thanking one person. Mark, I have to thank you because not only have you been my best friend and helped me to get to where I am today, but if it weren't for you I would not be in attendance tonight.*
>
> *I have never told you this but that day you stopped and helped me pick up my books you saved my life. That day was the last straw. I couldn't take it anymore. I was putting all my books away because my plan was to go home and take my life. I felt that no one even noticed I was alive so why did it matter if I was dead? And then you came around the corner and noticed me. You became my friend and you saved my life. Thank you, Mark. You are the reason I stand here.*

Mark and Joseph both went on to meet their wives, marry and have children. They remain friends even in their adult lives.

Your choices matter for generations. It's amazing to think that Mark's choice to stop and help Joseph changed history forever. One choice and Joseph is alive today and has children and will have grandchildren. Your choices matter for future generations.

CHAPTER 15

Tortured

The Death Railway

The construction of the Burma Railway (also known as the Death Railway) was considered one of the worst war crimes of the 20th century. It is a railway that stretches 258 miles from Bangkok, Thailand to Rangoon, Burma (now Yangon, Myanmar). This railway was constructed during World War II by the Empire of Japan.

Forced labor was used to build the railway. It's estimated that the Japanese military used about 180,000 Asian slaves and about 60,000 prisoners of war (POWs) to build it. The majority of the POWs were from Britain and Australia, and among them were about 350 American soldiers.

The conditions for the POWs and slaves were so horrific, words can never fully describe them. About 90,000 Asian slaves and more than 16,000 prisoners of war died during

141

the building of the Death Railway. Their diet consisted of a little rice and vegetables, served twice a day. They were forced to work sixteen or more hours a day. The Japanese motto was, "If you work hard you will be treated well; if you don't work hard you will be punished."

It was not uncommon to be working on the railway and get hit in the back of the head with the butt of a gun. Prisoners were punished for the smallest infractions.

Some of the punishments included kneeling on sharp sticks for hours while holding a boulder. They would tie prisoners up to trees with barbwire and leave them there for days with no food or water. There are stories of Japanese guards shoving water hoses into prisoner's mouths, filling their stomachs with water, then jumping on their enlarged bellies. Most prisoners died from this form of punishment.

There is a story recorded of one prisoner who tried to escape from the torture of the death railroad. He was gone for days before he was caught. They brought him back to the camp and beat him to the brink of death. They brought him before the other prisoners. They made him kneel down. The general unsheathed his sword and chopped off the prisoner's head. According to witnesses, the prisoner did not beg or plead for his life. It was as though he knew his fate and was ready for it to happen.

To me, the Death Railway is a horrible picture of what true torture is. Every day, you live with the knowledge that you could be beaten or killed. As was proven with the prisoner who attempted escape – there seemed to be no way out. So they just lived out their lives day in and day out, going nowhere.

The Mind Battle

So far, most of this book has focused on the physical things you need to do to get out of your rut, but in this chapter we will discuss the mind battle.

I fully understand the horror of the tortured mind and the part it plays in your recovery. I can't say it is anywhere close to the example of the torture that happened to those who built the Death Railway, but for a person suffering with a *tortured mind* it is all too real and horrible. It is even something that can bring death through suicide. I have known of those who chose the suicide route, due to their tortured minds.

> I fully understand the horror of the tortured mind and the part it plays in your recovery.

I too have dealt with what I call the tortured mind. In fact, it's relatively common with those who live a destructive lifestyle. I want you to know that you are not alone. Oftentimes it is your tortured mind that keeps you deep in the rut. You want to get better, but then it happens – the torture begins. Your mind starts to remind you of horrible moments in your life or things you have done. You hear voices telling you:

"You suck."

"Don't you remember those despicable things you've done?"

"You've gone too far to ever be any different."

It's real and it's a horrible torture to live through. There are also deeper parts to this torture, such as depression. I have a tortured mind that deals with depression. As I am writing this book, I can tell you that just a few short months ago, things were going great for me. I had received good news about our ministry and could see where God was taking us. I came home to my house that I never thought I could buy; I opened the door and my two beautiful children ran to me and jumped into my arms with all the excitement in the world. My wife came out of the kitchen looking as hot as ever, gave me a big kiss and asked me what I wanted for dinner.

Life was good. There was absolutely no reason to be depressed. We were actually at the point where we were coming out of that young married life of never having money to pay the bills. I really felt no stress at that point. Out of nowhere, I remember the distinct feeling of depression coming over me. I went into a few days of torture. I wanted to isolate. I felt down and tired. I didn't want to see anyone; and those old tortured mind thoughts started coming back into my head.

One afternoon, I was sitting in my living room. Annie and the kids were out shopping. I just felt so down and out. I thought to myself, "Why am I feeling so depressed when everything is going so good?"

And as I sat there, I heard a voice say, "You should just kill yourself." At that moment I pictured myself hanging in the garage and how that could actually happen.

Some of you reading this are thinking, "That is just crazy. Why would a guy who seems to have everything going right want to kill himself?"

There are others of you who know exactly what I am talking about. It's a torture that many live with – this torture of the mind that goes into emotions. I'd like to say that there's a quick fix and you just get free from it as soon as you're out of your rut of a destructive lifestyle. But there really isn't. It is a process.

Similar to the Death Railway

The tortured mind has many similarities to the Death Railway. Just like the prisoners on the railway, you have no idea at what point the punishment will come. At times, it's so bad there seems no way to escape except for death.

For many who built the infamous bridge and the railway, that was the case. It's estimated that one in five prisoners died building the Death Railway. It is said that an average of 38 people died for every kilometer of the railway that was built.

This is a complete guess of mine, but I bet that for every mile of highway in America, a person is lost to the torture of the mind. There are close to a million people a year who commit suicide. There are about three million, five hundred thousand square miles in the United States. So in the last three-and-a-half years, one person for every square mile of the United States has died from the torture of the mind.

Once the Death Railway was actually finished, the torture continued. The prisoner-workers were taken to POW camps where their torture continued. In the same way, even when you're out of your rut, the torture of your mind can continue.

The Torture Continues

One evening, I remember sitting in a pastor's conference where the guest speaker was talking about hearing from God. At the close, he asked each of us to sit in complete silence and listen for the voice of God to speak to us.

Now for a person who has dealt with a tortured mind for as many years as I have, the last thing I wanted to do was sit in silence. I sat there for a few minutes like the guest speaker had asked us to, and I almost went nuts. He asked people afterward to share what they heard in their silence. They went around the room with the microphone. People said things like,

"He said he loves me."

"He said he has great things for me."

"He said I am forgiven."

On and on they went. I was praying that the microphone would not come near me. I heard nothing like what the other people heard. In that silence, as I sat there, I heard what I will put into nicer words so you won't have to be privy to the cursing and the horrible accusations that came my way:

146

"You freaking suck!"

"You are a piece of junk!"

"Do you remember when you did this and did that?"

"If people ever found out who you really are, your ministry would be ruined."

"Why don't you just kill yourself?"

This is the mind torture I experienced almost ten years after getting out of my rut. I haven't been perfect in those ten years; there have been bumps in the road that made me fall back into the rut for a time. However, for most of those ten years, I was clear out of the rut. Yet still the mind torture was there.

Along the way, I have learned some major things on how to deal with the torture, and even to make it stop.

Speak Out When it Hits

For many years, when the torture came I wouldn't say anything to anyone and it would go on for months. I was so sure no one would understand. I also thought it would disqualify me for ministry if I said anything. I was so sure people would think I was nuts.

Back to Pastor Glenn's favorite saying:

"What you think disqualifies you is probably the one thing that does qualify you."

When I mustered the courage to speak out about this part of my bondage, people began to come to me for help with the same thing. I soon realized that many people struggle with a tortured mind.

Seek Help

I learned not only to speak out, but to also seek help. Now, when I'm feeling depressed, I tell Annie. While there isn't much she can do at that point, I discovered that simply saying it aloud to her brings a freedom to me. Knowing that Annie is aware somehow intensifies my resolve to pull out of the depression. Her encouragement is an immense help to me.

Finding the Root

Another thing I have learned about is what's called Theophostic Ministry. This is a ministry that teaches you to solve a problem by going to the root of it. Remember in Chapter 4, I said, "Every tree has a root."

In the area of mind torture, it tends to be the same old thing replaying over and over again in the mind. There has to be a root – a cause – and if you look back in your life, you can usually find it.

I have broken free from a lot of my mind torture by simply finding the root cause and dealing with it. I recommend doing this with a pastor or counselor. It always helps to have someone alongside you to help you face it and walk through it.

Knowing the Heart of God

Another thing I have found to help me with the torture of the mind is what I said earlier about knowing the *heart of God.* It took a long time for me to fully grasp this truth. (I'm *still* working on it.)

Once I understood the heart of the Father, I realized that none of the condemnation I was hearing came from Him. For years, incidents came back into my mind to haunt me about things I had done. When that happened I would pray and say, "I am so sorry God. Please, please forgive me of this sin." I did that over and over again.

I truly thought I was hearing the accusations from God, reminding me of all the bad things I'd done. But that wasn't God and it isn't His heart. He is very clear that our sins are thrown into the sea of forgetfulness (Micah 7:19). They are remembered no more. When I came to understand the heart of God, a lot of those old voices were quieted, because now I *knew* they weren't from God. I had uncovered the ruse of the enemy. God's voice is not the voice of accusation. His is the voice of love and compassion – and His voice is the only one that is important for me to hear.

God's voice is not the voice of accusation. His is the voice of love and compassion.

The torture of the mind is often the last vestige of the enemy's grasp when you're coming out of your rut. It is absolutely vital to your recovery to break free of that bondage.

You Are Not Alone

Many people start climbing out of their rut and then get hit with the thoughts of that tortured mind. They think they are the only one who has ever dealt with such issues. Since they think they are the only ones, they don't say anything, so the tortured mind defeats them and they go back into their rut.

I want you to know you are not alone. I have suffered from these attacks, and I have learned that I'm not alone. Since I started speaking on the bondage of a tortured mind, many people have come to me in tears saying, "I thought I was the only one."

It has been said that the survivors of the Death Railway never told their stories because the memories were so intensely painful. I can relate. I understand what it's like to not want to talk about your mind torture. But it's in the talking about it that dispels those voices.

I want to encourage you to find a compassionate, understanding pastor or counselor to walk through it with you. It's absolutely vital to getting out of your rut – and staying out.

CHAPTER 16

Small Beginnings

Have you ever heard the saying, "Don't despise the day of small beginnings"? (Zechariah 4:10)

I used to think that was something people said as a cop-out to make them feel better. Now I know different. Not only should you not despise small beginnings, you should actually *rejoice* in them. Small beginnings are biblical. Many of the history-changing people in the Bible came from humble, lowly beginnings.

The Story of Moses

Moses was born to a Jewish slave in Egypt. He was supposed to be killed with other male baby Jews as an order from the Pharaoh. His mother, a Jewish slave, had no idea what to do, but she knew she had to save her baby's life. So she wove a basket, put baby Moses in it, and then placed him in the Nile River.

This may have seemed a little crazy, but at least she knew he might have a chance to live. If she had kept him in the home, he would surely have been killed.

Baby Moses was discovered by none other than the Pharaoh's daughter – the princess of Egypt. She ordered her handmaidens to pull the basket out of the water, then she took Moses home and raised him as her own. Moses grew up in the palace of Egypt as a prince after being born a slave.

Later in life, Moses saw a Jewish slave being beaten by an Egyptian soldier. Moses knew his roots as a Jewish slave, even though he had grown up as a prince. Anger rose up in him and he killed the soldier. Once his crime was found out, he escaped and ran into the desert where he hid for years.

After forty years of living a nomadic life of a lowly shepherd out in the desert, Moses heard the voice of God speaking to him and telling him it was time to help set His people free.

Moses' response to God's call was something I find to be funny. He told God he couldn't do it because he stuttered. Moses, the stutterer, was being told to stand before the Pharaoh and demand that God's people be set free.

Eventually, after many warnings and plagues sent by God to the Egyptians, the Jewish slaves were released. Moses then led them – millions of people – out of bondage. Moses, a boy born to a slave, who was put into a basket and sent down the river, became a prince. Then he became the man God used to free an entire nation. Rejoice in small beginnings.

(You can read Moses' story in the first few chapters of the book of Exodus.)

The Story of Joseph

Another story of small beginnings is that of young Joseph. He started out as a shepherd boy who was despised by his older brothers. Their jealousy of Joseph – due to preferential treatment from their father – drove them to sell Joseph into slavery. He went through many hard years and adverse circumstances. Accusations came his way that questioned his character – one of which placed him into prison. But Joseph stayed strong and eventually became the top advisor to the king. He was placed in charge of all of the finances for the country. When famine came to the region, he was the one who saved the lives of those same brothers who had sold him to slavery. Rejoice in your small beginnings. (You can read this story in the last part of the book of Genesis – from Chapter 39 to the end.)

The Story of David

David was a shepherd boy. He was the youngest son of a man named Jesse. A prophet of God had told Jesse that one of his sons would be anointed to be the king of Israel. When the prophet came to anoint the chosen son of Jesse, the father lined up all his sons, but he hadn't bothered to even call David. Young David was out tending the sheep. That's how insignificant David appeared to his family.

He was not, however, insignificant to God. He was called of God to be a king. That little shepherd boy became the beloved king of Israel and was the *bloodline* through which Jesus the Messiah would be born. Rejoice in your small beginnings.

(The story of David is found in the Books of 1 and 2 Samuel.)

The Story of Jesus

Jesus of Nazareth was born in a manger – today, we would call it a barn. It was the place where the livestock was stabled. Jesus was born in a manger in the small town of Bethlehem. (If he ever left the front door open at home like I did when I was a kid, and his mother asked him, "Were you born in a barn?" He could say, "Yes, I was.")

This baby boy, who was born in a manger, became the Savior of the world. He was the Messiah; the King of Kings and the Lord of Lords; the one whose birth literally changed time forever. Jesus Christ was born in a lowly place, a place where no one would expect a king to be born. Rejoice in your small beginnings.

Small Beginnings in Business

Even in modern times, we find that small beginnings seem to build the most solid things. In the early eighties, there was a price war in the coffee industry. The major coffee brands were almost going bankrupt because of these price wars. The smaller companies struggled to sur-vive and many went under.

In the midst of the price war, a small company in Seattle, Washington, struggled to stand strong against huge companies like Folgers. This small company made a bold decision to quit the fight, but not to leave the war. They chose the road less traveled – a road no one had even thought of before. They opened a store where, instead of selling coffee by the can, they sold it by the cup. Then they got real gutsy and priced their cups of coffee dollars more than the other coffee companies were selling their cans full of coffee.

This company, through its very small beginnings, fought to become the best-known coffee in the world. The name? *Starbucks*. Rejoice in your small beginnings.

A Start-Over Is Not Easy

When coming out of a rut, you can't despise your small beginnings. It's where you will start. I've met so many people coming out of their rut who struggle with this. Once you leave your destructive lifestyle, you are basically starting a whole new life. It's a start-over and it will not be easy, but you can become a world changer like the people in the stories I just shared. Too many people really *do* despise their small beginnings. These are usually the ones who wind up staying in their rut.

These are the ones who come to me saying: "Jeremy, I need a job," "I need this," or "I need that." I will give them advice, but it's not always the advice they want to hear. In a world where you can watch a murder get solved in one hour on a CSI show, people expect big things to happen quickly.

A guy I knew was coming out of his rut. He called me and said, "I need a job." I told him of a company that was hiring.

His answer was, "Yeah I already talked to them, but they are only paying ten dollars an hour and it's not management."

I was blown away. This individual had done nothing to prove himself to anyone. He had only been clean for about forty days. I said to him, "Well what are you making now?"

He said, "Nothing, but I refuse to make ten dollars an hour."

Last I heard, this man is still in his rut and has never gotten his management job.

He could have gone down the street, taken the ten-dollar-an-hour job, and possibly moved up into management. But he despised small beginnings.

Not the Best Part of Town

When I first got out of Master's Commission, I applied at many churches to be a youth pastor. But every church that was hiring was not interested in hiring a guy who was clean off of cocaine for just over a year. I got frustrated and decided to go visit my parents in Alaska.

At that time, my father was the pastor of a small church in the inner city of Anchorage, Alaska. The area, called Mountain View (The View by locals), was not the best part of town. I love my dad so much and I'm proud of him for the churches he has gone to. He is a true risk-taker and he goes where not many pastors will go.

While there, I started wandering around Mountain View and quickly realized how ghetto it was. I had spent a lot of time in the *Bad Lands* of Philly and I saw that the gangsters in Mountain View were just as hard.

It's a crazy place. They had actually fenced this part of the city in and left only a few places where you could enter or leave. That way, when a crime is committed, they can barricade Mountain View until they find the perpetrator. Later I learned that many of the most wanted gang members from Los Angeles came to the Mountain View area to hide out.

The Mountain View Youth Group

Remember when I talked about *good* risks? This is one of those instances. I asked my dad if I could start a youth group at the church. I found another youth pastor, named Stephen, who had a bus and we decided to work together and reach the gangs and teens of Mountain View.

It was a slow start. I walked the streets of Mountain View for what would probably add up to weeks of time. I tried to let people know what I was doing in order to raise funds to help me reach these students. No one was interested in putting money towards our cause.

Finally, a franchise called Papa Murphy's Pizza offered to donate pizzas to my cause. This was just what I needed. Any youth pastor knows, free food is a great draw and I now had free pizza every week.

It had been a long battle but now I was excited. With free food, I was sure we would grow a youth group. I spread the word and handed out fliers. I remember standing in the church the first night, waiting for the multitudes to walk up. One kid arrived.

After awhile I thought, "Well, this is Alaska. They're probably cold. I bet Pastor Stephen's bus is full."

Pastor Stephen pulled up and on that bus there were six kids – all under the age of twelve. I had ten pizzas for six kids.

I went out and preached to those seven kids like it was a conference of ten thousand.

I walked to the back of the church, hid in a closet and started crying. I cried out to God: "I've been walking these streets. I've gotten free pizza. I prepared the service and prepared my sermon. I've done all I know how to do! There are seven kids, all under the age of twelve! I am a youth pastor, not a children's pastor!" (I later learned that two of the kids were four years old!)

Continuing my pity party, I said, "God I refuse to go out there and preach to these little kids!"

In that moment, as I sat there whining and feeling sorry for myself, I heard God say, "If you are too big to go and minster to those kids, you are too small for me to ever use again."

I picked myself up and thought, "Well, I'm sure not going back to my old lifestyle."

I went out and preached to those seven kids like it was a conference of ten thousand. I was wondering what I was going to do with all those pizzas when one of the kids (after we'd eaten) looked at me and said, "Pastor, we don't get to eat like this through the week. You think we could take some pizza home with us?"

I let each one of them take pizza home that night. When they were gone, I broke down in tears again. This time it was not because I was sad, but because I almost missed the point of all the work I did. Those children that came out were hungry and hadn't eaten well in a long time. At least for that one night, they and their families were fed.

I went back to Papa Murphy's and said, "I'm going to need more pizzas. We have hungry kids." I had no idea how many pizzas I would need.

Willie and the Sons of Samoa

Just a few weeks after our small start, I ran into a guy named Willie. Willie was in a gang known as the "Sons of Samoa." He was one of the top members in The View. I stopped and talked to him. He said, "You're that crazy white boy everyone has been talking about."

I said, "Yep that's me. I'm just walking around letting people know that Jesus loves them."

He said, "That's great; does he love me enough to get me a job?"

I said, "I'm sure we can help."

I had no idea how I was going to help Willie find a job. He was a big, scary looking Samoan with tons of tattoos.

He'd only recently been released from prison, so he had a record. But Willie had five kids and all he knew was the hustle. He had no job skills. Finally, after I made many phone calls, I found someone willing to train him in a trade.

The next Wednesday, I got my pizzas and got ready for my seven kids to show up – but it wasn't just seven kids that showed up. Close to two hundred Samoans from the Sons of Samoa filled my church.

Some preachers would have been scared and put up metal detectors, but not my dad or me. We let them come and be who they were. I grew to love all the people in that youth group. I say *people* because our youth group ranged from four-year-olds to thirty-four-year-olds.

Every Wednesday from then on, we could
expect one hundred to two hundred Samoans
to come have church with us.

Every Wednesday from then on, we could expect one hundred to two hundred Samoans to come have church with us. I still love and miss my SOS family. They taught me so much about ministry. But most importantly, they taught me to *rejoice in small beginnings*.

CHAPTER 17

Know Your Gift

The Losing Contestants

Have you ever watched those singing competitions on TV – like *American Idol* and others? You listen as contestants stand there looking totally serious about their future in the music industry. And yet when they start to sing, you cringe. It sounds more like a cat when someone steps on its tail. You don't know whether to laugh or just roll your eyes.

The response of the judges is something like: "Do you really think you're a good singer?" Some of them genuinely do and others just seem to love music.

It always ends the same way. They're told they will not be moving on to the next round. That's when they throw a huge temper tantrum, declaring that the judges (who have made millions in the music industry) have no idea what they're talking about. The so-called singer then leaves the room in tears, into the arms of a family member who continues to assure the losing contestant how amazing a singer he or she truly is.

I Love Music; I Love to Sing

No one can deny that these folks probably truly love music. I am right there with them. I love all types of music, and I love listening to it and singing along. If you get into my car, you'll see I have an eclectic collection of worship, rock, rap, country, hard rock, and even some Frank Sinatra. I love all types of music and I love to sing. I sing all the time, but I've come to realize that as much as I love music and love to sing, I would, without a doubt, be that losing contestant on the music show.

When I sing, Annie lovingly giggles at me as I make up my own words to the songs because I can't remember the right ones. My favorite place to sing is in the shower. (Typical, right?) Sometimes she'll come and shut the door from our bedroom to the master bath because she just can't take the wild tunes that are emanating from the shower.

Finding Your Gifts

When climbing out of your rut, it's very important to find your gifts. What I mean by a "gift" is your God-given talent that you are good at and enjoy. We all have a gift (or gifts). The first thing I want to make clear is, just because you love something doesn't mean that it is a gift. I love so many things that aren't really my gift.

I Should Have Taken Lessons

A few years ago, I decided I needed to find fun things to do in my new life outside of the old rut. I received an invitation to go to Colorado to go snowboarding. I accepted the invitation thinking, "Ah, this will be easy." I couldn't have been more wrong. The only easy part was the ski lift.

Of course being the risk-taker that I am, I decided to jump in with both feet. Literally. I went right past the bunny slope, past the blue diamond, and on up to the blacks. I mean, if you're going to learn how to snowboard, you start out on the hardest slopes, right? Well that's what I did.

> When climbing out of your rut, it's very important
> to find your gifts.

I came to the place where I was supposed to get off the ski lift, which had very kindly taken me to the top of the mountain. I put the snowboard to the ground and it slid right out from underneath me. The problem with that was the fact that my feet were strapped to the snowboard, so they went with the board. Bottoms up!

This is when I learned about that embarrassing skiing mistake where they have to stop the entire ski lift, with hundreds of people riding it, so that one poor soul – who thought it was best to learn by jumping in – could pick himself up and get out of the way.

It didn't take me long to learn that I should have taken a few lessons before taking on the black diamond slopes. After multiple falls, watching the good skiers pass me three or four times on their trips up and down the hill, and about three hours later, I finally made it to the bottom. My bruised ego and bottom were done for the day.

Today, after many snowboarding trips, it has become one of my favorite pastimes. I go as much as I possibly can.

I'm quick to add that as much as I love to snowboard, you won't be seeing me at the *X Games* anytime soon. I love it, but I am still known for a good wipeout. You will see no jumping or rail grinding from me. I love snowboarding but it's most definitely not one of my gifts. There's no way I could ever make money at it.

My Primary Gifts

I have learned that one of my primary gifts is that of sales and marketing. I have never taken any college classes for sales or marketing, but I never really had to. I love sales and marketing, so I study it.

I enjoy seeing the reactions of people through sales and marketing. This is most definitely a gift I have. I am creative and also can sell just about anything. It is something I have made a lot of money at. It took me awhile to understand this gift and I did many jobs that I hated. Then one day I got a sales job and realized that I never wanted to work at an hourly job again.

Every sales job I have taken, I have been one of the top salespeople and all the while, I never felt like I was working hard. When I got into a marketing job, I moved up directly under the owner of the company. He recognized my talents and even used my advice in the operation of several of his companies.

I love marketing and I'm good at it. It's more fun than work for me. This is what it means to understand your gifting and to operate in it.

Your Gift Can Be Lucrative

Each person on the planet has certain giftings and talents that they are especially good at. It's usually something that, when applied correctly, can become lucrative for that individual.

In our society, we are taught to go to school and get an education so we can get a good job and make lots of money. In a way, that's right, but it misses a crucial element – discovering the one thing that is your gift.

It's that thing in life that you can do better than most anyone else you know. The sad thing is, many times people take their *gift* and put it in the hobby section of life. I believe that's why studies show that eighty percent of people hate what they do for a living by the time they reach the age of thirty.

Again, this is why you can't despise small beginnings. Even if you learn your gift and recognize it, it takes time to build it into something that can earn an income. It's important that you find your gift, and I promise when you do, you *can* make money with it.

On this journey, it will be important for you to find other people who can help you in your gift. How I wish I had had someone to mentor me when I was in high school.

In my present role as a youth pastor, I've made it my goal to help teenagers find their gifts so they can live a life that impacts the world forever. The people who make the greatest impact in their world are the ones who find their gift and make it their life.

How About Carpentry?

If I had met me as a kid I would have told me that there was a possibility to make money with my sales skills.

All of my teachers and counselors knew I was an outgoing person who could influence people to go my way. This is why I was constantly in the principal's office – I could never shut up and I always got the entire class stirred up. But my counselors, as nice as they were, didn't pick up on my gift.

I'll never forget the day I got kicked out of my Spanish class. The teacher, in no uncertain terms, stated that she did not want to see me back for the rest of the semester.

I remember sitting in the office of my counselor. She said something like this: "Jeremy, it doesn't look like you'll ever go to college, so we need to find you something to do with your life. I am enrolling you in carpentry class for your afternoons here at school."

If any of my friends are reading this book, at this point they are now rolling on the floor in hysterical laughter. I am the absolute worst when it comes to building or fixing anything. I have perhaps *three* tools in my entire house and anytime I use them I break something.

The rest of my year in carpentry class was absolutely horrible. Our assigned job was to each finish a miniature house that fit the code for a real home. When finished, our homes would be the size of a small shed. My shed leaned at an angle and if anyone walked into it the whole thing would fall.

Funny Follow-Up

Here's an interesting (funny) follow-up fact. Many years later, in Oklahoma, I tried to fix a barn. The horse stall I attempted to add to the barn had the *same exact lean* as my high school carpentry class project.

My friend, Gerry, dubbed it, "The Philadelphia Lean." This is what the ranchers around Oklahoma call me. Anytime I come out to their ranch they yell, "Philadelphia, don't you go breaking anything." (Calling me Philadelphia is their loving way of calling me a city boy.) They must love me, because I've broken many things on ranches around here and yet I'm still welcome.

Now you can see how ludicrous it was for a counselor to even suggest that I could ever choose carpentry as a way to make a living. It's nowhere close to being my gift, and yet she suggested that that was what I should spend my life doing. Scary.

Gifting Test

I encourage you to find your own gift. It'll be something you love and something you're good at. How do you know you're good at something? If people other than you, especially the people who love you most, say you are good at something, it's a good chance you are.

Another great way to discover your giftings and talents is to take a *gifting test*. (Yes, there really is such a thing.) You can find them online; most colleges have them, and; oftentimes, professional counselors will administer such tests.

We actually have these kinds of tests available at my home church, Destiny Life Church. It's a goal at our church to help believers find their destiny – and in order to find your destiny you must know your gift.

After you have found something you love and are good at, find someone who makes money doing what you love and learn from them.

When starting out, if you believe you have *nothing to learn,* you are in trouble. Having read much of my story at this point, it probably will not surprise you to know that there was a point when I thought I didn't have anything to learn.

Then I began to network with people who were doing what I wanted to do and were making money at it. I submitted to learn from them. What a difference that made in my life.

Find someone who is making money doing the thing that you love to do; you will learn so much from them. If they are earning an income and you are not, they are a professional and you are an amateur.

Learning vs. Competing

Here's another possible roadblock: Human nature makes you want to *compete* with someone who is in the same field of endeavor. I know, because I am a very competitive person. However, I received this good advice and it served me well.

When you find something you love, and you find the person who is the best at making money doing it, get close to them and learn. Don't compete with them; soak up their knowledge and their expertise. Find out how you can help. Don't ask for pay; don't think you need to show off. Be humble. Get near them, make yourself valuable, and learn everything you can.

As you learn to gravitate toward great people,
you too will become great.

Once you find your gift and begin to function in it, you won't have to fight for your place; you will find it. Very often, the student becomes the teacher just as a process of natural progression.

Of course, when you find your gifts, it doesn't mean you can ignore your faults. On the other hand, it's a huge mistake to concentrate on your faults more than your gifts. If you have a fear of failure, you will wind up concentrating on all your faults that could trip you up. That behavior pattern will prevent you from becoming good at what you love.

As you learn to gravitate toward great people, you too will become great. Keep in mind that while your gift may be similar to another person's, it is still unique to you. That's why as Christians we are called, "the Body of Christ" (1 Corinthians 12:27).

Because so many people look with envy at the gifts of others, we wind up with *hands* wanting to be *feet.* If the hands are all worried about walking, and if they don't leave that to the feet, they will never be the best hands they can be.

As I mentioned, I'm good at sales and marketing, but I am horrible at administration and detail work. You would not want me to do your accounting or organize your file cabinet because it's not my skill. You can find many people who absolutely love math and numbers. They would be great to hire to do your accounting, but I am not that guy.

Now imagine if I spent most of my life trying to make myself good at accounting, simply because someone told me that CPAs make great money. Think of how frustrated I'd be. And yet this happens all the time.

How to Balance

Here is how I balance it all out. I consider my weaknesses and make sure they don't hurt me. In other words, it's not a weakness that I need to work on or improve; it's a weakness in that it's *not my strong gift.*

At this point in my life, I have learned how to create an Excel spreadsheet; I know how to read and prepare a budget. I'm even getting better with detail work. For the most part though, I realize there are people who are better at it than I am. If possible, I let them do it so I can con-centrate on getting better at what I love. This is why we need a team.

The only way I'm going to become good at something is to discover what I love to do – and what I'm good at doing – and line that up to create my destiny.

My hope and prayer for you is that you find what you love to do and find ways to make money at it. Only then will you live your life *alive* and out of a rut.

This is actually the life God has planned for us. He gives us gifts so we can all be the best at something. Every indi-vidual has his or her own unique gift – I promise. I've met people from all over the world and without fail, every one of them has a gift that other people would be willing to pay for. Obviously some gifts will earn a greater income than others. CPAs are probably making a greater income than I do as a youth pastor.

I have to quickly add that it's not all about making the most money. Doing what you love means living a life of fulfillment. You're doing what makes you excited to be alive rather than hating going to work each day.

Matthew Barnett, Pastor of the Los Angeles Dream Center, in his book *The Cause Within You* (a great book to help you in your gift-finding process), says this:

> *When you realize that you are wonderfully unique, you can start making a one of a kind contribution to the world.*

You are unique and you do have a God-given gift that can help you reach any dream. Know that your gift is something you can do better than anyone else, and you can use it to live life *alive* – outside of the rut.

CHAPTER 18

Thanks Carter

During the summer before my senior year in high school, in 1996, my parents moved from Philadelphia to Anchorage, Alaska. They saw the trouble I was getting into and tried to move me as far away as possible.

By this time, I was already into heavy drugs on a daily basis, was in a serious relationship with a girl, and was getting into numerous fights. I was arrested for the first time during my junior year.

At first, I was angry at my parents. I didn't want anything to do with Alaska, but since then, Alaska has become very close to my heart. It is one of the most amazing places I have ever lived, and I met many wonderful people there—many of whom are still in my life today.

My Friend, Aaron

One of those was my good friend, Aaron Becker. Aaron moved back with me to Philadelphia after graduation and went through a lot of the same mess I did. He has since come out of his rut and went on to become a Marine who served our country in Iraq. He is now a firefighter and police officer in Alaska, in addition to being an amazing father. I am proud to call him my friend and want to give a big *thank you* to him right here for always protecting me (due to my loud mouth on the streets of Philly). I owe you, Aaron.

A Spiritual Father

Another key person I met in Alaska was Carter Eby. Carter was the youth pastor at a local church in the area. I didn't have any friends when I moved there and I needed to meet girls. I heard his youth group was the hopping one, so I decided to visit. Carter Eby was the first person beyond my father to show me the love of a true spiritual father. He was always there for me and still is. Even when I went through my craziest of crazy times as a drug addict, Carter would call me and tell me that God had a plan for my life. Carter not only taught me about God, he also taught me about life – about practical things.

He taught me the importance of being debt free and having money before you bought things. The crazy thing is, Carter was a youth pastor who didn't make much money, yet he had boats, four wheelers, snow machines, and a big house. He attained all of this by making right choices. He taught me the importance of making right choices.

Good Character Can Win Any Fight

Carter talked a lot about being a man of your word. Everywhere you go in Anchorage, Alaska, Carter Eby is known as a person who would never do anyone wrong. I got good jobs from dropping his name. I messed some of them up too, but he still stayed friends with those businesses because of his integrity.

Carter Eby was the first person beyond my father
to show me the love of a true spiritual father.

This is crucial when getting out of the rut of a destructive lifestyle. If you don't want to learn the hard way, then be a man or woman of your word. Don't lie. Tell the truth even when it hurts and if you let someone down, or make a mistake. Apologize and then make amends.

Carter taught me how to love people, even when they didn't deserve it. I saw many people do things to him that deserved getting called out. In the natural realm, they probably deserved to get whipped up on, but he never repaid in kind.

I've run into some pretty big fighters in my life. People who have said horrible things about me because they wanted to take me out of a position they wanted, or simply because they didn't like me and wanted to see me hurt. I've had people try to fight with me because they thought they were right when they really weren't.

I could have fought with all of them. I could have made that costly mistake. But Carter helped me see that life isn't about being the best fighter. Life is about being the person who stands the longest and the strongest. Your good character can win any fight without you saying a thing. This is why it's important to be a person of your word.

One of the most important things Carter ever taught me was to learn at least three things – in addition to my dream – that could earn an income for me. Every week, we met at Kaladi Brothers Coffee Shop (the greatest coffee in the world) and talked.

I remember one particular morning when we were at the coffee shop chatting. This was in 2003, after I had come out of rehab and finished my time at Master's Commission. I had returned to Alaska to visit my parents and decided to stay and start the youth group.

"It's crucial that you are able to support yourself while you're waiting for your dreams to materialize."

During that conversation, Carter said, "Being a youth pastor is your dream, right?"

"Yes, of course it is," I answered.

"That's good, Jeremy, but since you aren't making money at your dream yet, I want to encourage you to learn at least three other things that can earn an income for you." Then he added, "It's crucial that you are able to support yourself while you're waiting for your dreams to materialize."

Learn Skills That Will Support You

That was awesome advice and I now want to pass it along to you. This goes right along with the previous chapter regarding finding your gift. Many times, once you discover your gift and you are putting your dreams and desires in place, you're on the right track, but it can still take time for that dream to become profitable. This also fits in with my point about not despising small beginnings.

When you have a dream, you have to be willing to volunteer at it until you have the opportunity to make money from it. While working on your dream, take the time to learn other skills that will support you on your way to the dream. Like Carter told me, it's good to learn other things that can earn a sufficient income. It's something you can put on your resume at any time to make money.

I am secure right now in my youth pastor job, but if I ever lost my paycheck in that position, I could do it on a volunteer basis and still earn a living. I took Carter's advice and learned other skills and I know I can always get a job.

I have a commercial driver's license and can drive a tractor trailer. I can install cable in homes. And as I mentioned before, I'm accomplished in sales and marketing.

Looking back, I believe Carter Eby's advice helped me stay out of my rut. Because I've made myself valuable with skilled work, I was never forced to go back to hustling out of desperation for cash. I could always earn a living for myself.

My first youth ministry in Alaska was on a volunteer basis. During that time, I worked in sales and cable installation as well as a night job at a home improvement store. Eventually I had enough experience to get paid to be a youth pastor. Yet I still had those skills to fall back on.

I never discounted or belittled my volunteer work. To this day, I feel my volunteer work provided me with some of the most fulfilling experiences I ever had.

So there you have it. Learn three skills besides your dream that can support you financially. It will give you a sense of worth and value in addition to preventing a calamitous slide back down into the pit.

As an added note –

I didn't go to truck driving school. I found a truck driver who was willing to teach me.

I didn't go to cable installation school. I found a person who was willing to teach me.

I didn't go to sales and marketing school. I found people who were willing to teach me. I also did a lot of studying on my own.

You can do this too. It's not rocket science. Someday you'll also say, "Thanks Carter."

CHAPTER 19

Never Quit

Back into the Mess

Following my terrifying experience with the aneurysm in 1999, I was confined to my apartment for about six months. I was absolutely and hopelessly depressed. I wasn't allowed to drive. My parents had long since gone back to Alaska. I was pretty much at the mercy of other people. And human nature being what it is, after a while, people forget. They get busy with their own lives. The friend who was stranded and cooped up in his apartment was no longer high on their list of priorities.

As I sat there day after day, I knew I was going back into a deep depression. It wasn't easy, because due to the aneurysm, my life had changed forever. I had lost some of my eyesight and I was experiencing extreme headaches.

The only way I can describe them is, it felt like someone was shoving a knife into the side of my temple and then twisting. All I could do when the pain hit was curl up in a ball and pray that I could go to sleep.

At that point, the doctors told me that I might have to deal with seizures for the rest of my life. They still were not sure if I would ever get full feeling back in my left arm and leg.

Of course, I should have been thankful just to be alive and not paralyzed; but when you're heading into depression you can't see the good in anything. I knew I had promised God that I would get my life straight. I sat there dreaming of speaking to young people, telling them my story so they wouldn't have to go through what I did. I knew I had a call on my life. Still, it all looked hopeless.

I knew I had a call on my life.
Still, it all looked hopeless.

I know many of you learn-the-hard-way folk can definitely relate. You lie there in your rut – usually while you're causing pain for all the people around you – and you're dreaming of the day that you can *help people*. Crazy.

I have come to realize that most people in the rut actually have huge hearts, some of the biggest I have ever seen. The reason they can't get out of their rut is because *they haven't learned how*. That was me as I sat there in that house. I wanted so bad to do good, but I didn't know where to plant my feet. So I ended up going right back to my mess.

A friend of mine came by to visit me and see how I was doing. I asked him if he had any coke on him. He looked at me as if I were crazy. "Dude, your brain just exploded – the last thing you should be doing is some blow."

I didn't care. I just wanted to feel better and knew no other way to do it at that point. Being the salesman that I am, I convinced him to give me some. At that point, I made a wholesale slide right back into the pit. A few months later, I hit rock bottom.

As I sat there all alone, I became so depressed that my mind told me there was no way I would ever fulfill my dreams. I believed that lie and I *quit trying*.

Don't Ever Quit

What I know now that I didn't know then, is to never ever quit. No matter what – don't ever quit.

A few years later, as I sat in that rehab center filling out the application for Master's Commission, I started praying. I knew struggles were going to come; I knew I would go through hard times. But I prayed like this:

"God, I may fall as I travel on this journey, but I refuse to fail again. I won't quit on you like I did in that house."

Let me tell you, the struggles came. I experienced moments where it seemed there was no hope at all. I took a few bad falls. But every time, I got back up.

Have you ever seen the classic movie, *Rudy*? I *love* that movie! Read that, I LOVE that movie.

It is based on the true story of a young man who grew up in a middle class neighborhood near the Notre Dame campus. He was short and built small; just looking at him, you would never think of him as a college football player. But Rudy had a dream. He had a deep-seated desire to play football for the Fighting Irish of Notre Dame.

> What I know now that I didn't know then, is to never ever quit. No matter what – don't ever quit.

Rudy is an individual who refused to fail. Scenes in the movie show huge football players taking him down like a semi-truck hitting a Mini Cooper. Rudy, bloody and beaten, gets hit over and over again, but he never stays down. Each and every time, he jumped back up and got back on the line for the next play.

This is what I have learned to do in my life. When I fall, I get right back up. None of us are perfect and you definitely won't be when you're coming out of your rut. You'll make colossal mistakes. You'll fall down. But you determine in your mind that a fall is not the same as *failing.* Don't lie there. Pick yourself up and never quit.

Countless times, I have wanted to just lie down and die – but then the memories of all my years of *learning the hard way* would come flooding back. I knew I didn't want to go back there. But more importantly, I would remember my promise to God when I told Him I would never quit.

Priorities Out of Whack

Several years ago, I was at a point where I felt as though I had made it. I was the youth pastor for what many considered one of the flagship churches for the Assemblies of God in Oklahoma. I stood in a position that many people had said I would never attain. I was a youth pastor at a big church.

I know. Big deal, right? You have to remember, I was still dealing with my rut. Like I said, your gift will sometimes take you places where your character's not quite ready for. I was still battling heavy stuff in my own mind. So much so, I came to the place where I had to step down as youth pastor of that church.

I was giving so much to what I *thought* was my *cause* that I forgot all about what God had called me to do as a father and husband. My priorities were all out of whack and my marriage suffered because of it. I went from proving everyone wrong to proving everyone right.

A few weeks later, I found myself sitting at my new job as a car salesman at a local dealership. Oh, the intense humiliation of having people I once pastored come to the car lot to check up on me to see how I was doing. I'm not sure which was more humiliating – the fact that people came to see how I was doing, or that out of a church of over a thousand, only a very few did.

So I sat at my new job freaking out about how I was going to pay the rent for my family. My thoughts went something like this:

"I can't believe I'm in my mid-twenties and I've already screwed up my chance to change the world for God."

I went into this monstrous pity party and began to hate life all over again. I'd been through so much, and I thought I was out of the learning-the-hard-way pattern, but at that moment, it seemed that all of my dreams had been snatched away from me.

That pity party lasted almost two months. Throughout that time, I kept hearing God tell me, "You said you would never quit." After about two months of hearing that, I realized I had a decision to make. I may have fallen but I didn't have to fail. I could pick myself up.

The Open Door

So after that wake-up call, the next day was easy, right? I wish life were really like that. The pity party may have been over, but the difficult time lasted almost two years. Finally, God opened the door for the job I mentioned previously, where I started working in marketing and sales. It was the perfect job for me.

The company was Resource One. It's a company that non-profit organizations look to for help in raising funds. This company is very good at what it does. I learned a great deal about ministry while working for them. To my great joy, God promoted me in that company. I got back my old spark and knew then that I was *not* going to fail.

It was at Resource One that I met Matt Moore, who has since become a very close friend. I shared with him an idea I had – my dream about a certain type of media ministry. He loved the idea and helped me bring it to reality. Before I knew what was happening, I was back in the ministry with The SOZO Movement.

It has been awesome to watch The SOZO Movement grow the way it has. Still, I had a deep desire to get back to my dream of helping youth on a daily basis. I wanted to help them avoid having to learn the hard way – the way I did.

Prophetic Words of Wisdom

I will never forget the day I had lunch with Matthew Barnett, lead pastor of the LA Dream Center. I was giving him a pitch on how Resource One could help the LA Dream Center. I was in mid-sentence when he stopped me and said, "When are you going to go back to being a pastor?"

No, I didn't start crying at that moment, but I almost did. What he said was what I wanted with all my heart. He had nailed it perfectly.

After that meeting with Pastor Matthew, I began to send my resume to a few places, but it seemed no one was interested in me. After a time of being rather frustrated, I talked to my pastor, Lloyd Ziegler.

"What am I doing wrong?" I asked him.

Pastor Z said, "The problem is, you're looking for a *pastor-job.* God wants to give you a *home* from which you will minister."

Now that was a profound statement. And prophetic as well.

So I quit sending out the applications and resumes. I just stopped. I said, "God, I will not quit on you. I'll wait on you and I'll be happy where I am – working for Resource One and building The SOZO Movement."

The funny thing was, it was an awesome gig. I wouldn't have chosen to work anywhere else, but I wanted to live my dream again.

My dream guaranteed I'd experience a drop in pay; my dream guaranteed I'd no longer fly around on private jets like I was doing with Resource One. But man, I desperately wanted my dream. With all my heart, I wanted my dream.

Destiny Life Church

During this time, even though we were living in the Tulsa area, I considered my home church to be Relevant Life, in Dallas, because that is where Pastor Zeigler was the lead pastor. Even though it was four-and-a-half hours away, it was still home for me and Annie and we attended as often as we could.

One week, I was preparing to leave for Washington, DC, for a conference for Resource One. That meant I couldn't drive to Dallas that weekend. On the spur of a moment, Annie and I decided we would visit a church right down the street from us.

We had learned that it was merging with another church that Sunday. It's always fun to watch two churches *trying* to merge – you know, where the people are fighting over the place they sit every Sunday. Who is the head usher? This guy or the other guy? But when we arrived at the church, I didn't see any of this. All I saw was amazing people who were super-friendly.

As we walked in, they didn't just greet us, but genuinely wanted to get to know us. I was blown away. I remember leaning over to Annie and saying, "How did we not know about this place, Destiny Life Church?"

Looking around the congregation, I saw people that I knew. I saw Bob and Debbie Diskerud, who had been pastors on staff at a church I was connected with in Alaska.

I listened to Pastor Glenn Shaffer speak, and listening to him made me want to get to know him and learn from him. Annie and I had no idea at that moment that Pastor Glenn and his wife, Ami, would become some of the most amazing and life-changing people in our lives. Oh, and one more thing – we had no idea they were looking for youth pastors to hire.

After months of praying and talking extensively with Pastor Glenn and Ami, we accepted the youth pastor position at Destiny Life Church. Pastor Lloyd Zeigler was right on – we found not just a job, but a *home*. Huge difference!

From that part of my journey, I learned to never, ever quit. If you don't quit, your dreams *will* come to pass. I could have laid it all down at that car dealership and accepted it as my life. I could have quit on my dream.

God Restores

I want to quickly add here that I don't mean to suggest that working at a car dealership is a bad thing. I have many close friends who sell cars. They love what they do and they make a ton of money. But that was not my dream! Your dream is what makes you come alive.

When you are coming out of your rut, you may fall down but you need not fail. Even if it takes years to get back up – like it did for me multiple times in my life – God is good and He *restores*. The only person that can take you out of your calling is **you**.

Keep Getting Back Up

Herschel Walker is known as one of the greatest NFL running backs of all time. He held the record for "most yards gained" for many years. He is a true champion and remembered for his greatness.

The interesting thing about the career of this champion, who ran more yards than anyone else in his day, is that his average run was 4.3 yards. That's correct. Herschel Walker fell every 4.3 yards, on average.

So what's the point? The point is, he is not remembered for how many times he fell, but rather for how many times he *got up*. Imagine his career if he would have quit after that first fall at 4.3 yards. He would have never even been remembered as a great NFL player.

He did *not* quit at that first fall. He got back up, ran, and fell again. He got back up, ran, and fell again. He was remembered as one of the greatest players because he just kept getting back up.

You *will* fall. That's a promise. The question is, *will you get back up?* Just because you fall *doesn't mean you have to fail!* You don't have to lose. It's your choice.

You never have to go back to learning the hard way. You can get out of your rut. Promise yourself today that you will not quit on yourself. No matter what other people around you may say, you refuse to quit.

One of my mentors, Jeanne Mayo, has a quote that I love:

> **"Don't surrender your dreams due to the noisy negatives around you."**

Don't worry about what others are saying about you. This is your life; this is about you and your dreams.

You will fall, but please don't fail. Don't ever quit. I promise you, the joy that will come is so much more than anything you will find in that life of addictions and destruction.

I can't wait to hear your story of how you became a champion.

CHAPTER 20

You're His Favorite

Made Me Feel Special

During my growing up years, my grandfather was my very best friend. I looked up to him and admired him. Almost every summer, I stayed with him and my grandma. I explained in Chapter 3 that they owned a restaurant and bar near Cleveland, Ohio.

Staying with my grandparents was one of my favorite things to do, because they knew how to make me feel special. They lived in an apartment above the restaurant which was known as the Fiesta Restaurant. It was located on Main Street in Kent, Ohio. Even though it was called the Fiesta, they didn't serve anything on the menu that even resembled Mexican food. But did they ever serve good food. My grandma was the cook at the restaurant for thirty-five years. In my mind, she is still the best cook alive today.

We did many things together. Grandpa would often take me out fishing on Lake Erie. Because he had a dream to see the Space Shuttle go up, he and I made the journey to Florida to see a launch.

I'll never forget when we were on our way to Florida, we stopped in Atlanta to visit one of my grandpa's old friends. We pulled up in my grandpa's new Cadillac, which was his pride and joy. No one else, not even Grandma, was allowed to drive it.

===

"You must be your Grandpa's favorite."

===

Grandpa's friend was a retired cop and, in my eyes he was a giant. He was always a little scary to me as a kid because half of one his hands was missing. His wife had shot it off in an argument. (Scary thought.)

When we pulled up to his house, the ex-cop came walking out to the car. I was sitting in the front seat of Grandpa's Cadillac eating crackers. I'm sure there were crumbs everywhere. He extended that scary half-of-a-hand through my rolled down window and said with a laugh, "You must be your Grandpa's favorite."

That scene and those words were from that moment on, indelibly etched in my mind. I already believed I was his favorite, and this man's words only served to confirm it.

I Was the *Frog*

Grandpa knew how to make me feel like a superstar. His nickname for me was "Frog." (Believe me; I made sure he was the *only one* allowed to call me Frog!) At one point, he bought a little stuffed frog and gave it to me. That frog was more than special to me. From the moment he gave it to me, I carried it with me wherever I went.

You may be wondering why call anyone his grandkid "Frog." If you're old enough, you may remember the song, "Joy to The World," by the group, Three Dog Night. The first line of lyrics went:

Jeremiah was a bullfrog, he was a good friend of mine...

Jeremiah – Jeremy – to Grandpa it was close enough. He designated that song as *my song.* He had a rule in his bar. When a live band was in there playing a gig, no matter what song they were playing at the time, when I walked in the door they had to stop that song and start playing "Joy to the World" (the first line at least). Do you think that wasn't a heady experience for a little kid? I loved it.

Every year, Grandpa had a calendar made with my current school picture on the front. That calendar hung in the bar all year long – right up there for everyone to see.

I always sat at his favorite table and ate dinner with him. He would say the same thing whenever I sat down. First he would say, "You don't love me anymore do you?"

My quick reply was always: "Of course I love you, Grandpa."

He would lean over to me and come back with: "Frog, you're my favorite. I hope you know that."

Now that I'm an adult, I can look back and be pretty sure he said that to all his grandkids. At that moment, I never thought about that. It just meant so much for me to hear him say that I was his favorite.

Grandpa's DNR Request

It was around my twelfth birthday that Grandpa got very sick. They didn't have the medical technology then that they have today. He suffered from a stroke and it looked like he would not be able to live a quality life after that, so he signed a *Do Not Resuscitate* (DNR) form – as I mentioned in Chapter 4. Only a few days later, this amazing man passed away.

Later in my life, as I walked through my hard times of addictions and the bottomless ruts, when someone called me a screw up or tell me I was hopeless, I pulled out my beloved stuffed frog. I held it close to remind myself that I was my grandpa's favorite. When the hardest of the hard times came, I knew that at least Grandpa was proud of me. Many, *many,* times the frog was virtually *all* I had to cling to.

Rest assured, when I was the mean tough guy on the streets, using and dealing, *no one* knew I was packing a stuffed frog. It was one of my most closely guarded secrets.

193

The very last time they arrested me and took me to rehab, I lost nearly all my possessions. That included my beloved stuffed frog – Grandpa's special gift to me.

The Truth That Set Me Free

In rehab, I learned an amazing truth that set me forever free. As much as I *thought* I needed that frog, I came to realize I no longer needed it. I no longer had to keep forcing myself to remember that I was Grandpa's favorite. I learned that I am *God's favorite*. What a revelation!

I learned that I am *God's favorite*. What a revelation!

He whispers that truth to my heart all the time. He has shown me, and continues to show me, through my life's journey, in all that He's has done for me. I no longer need a stuffed frog to cling to in order to establish my identity and my sense of worth. I have the Creator God of the universe as my *Daddy.*

I heard God speak to me and tell me I am His favorite. No matter how many times I've fallen, He has picked me up again. He has let me see many of my dreams come to fruition. I'm sure I'll see more as I head happily into a promising future.

He is there when I start to feel myself go into a depression or when one of the headaches comes on. But even more than that, it's what He has done for me.

I rejected God for many years. I even told people I wanted nothing to do with Him. One night, I was sitting in a bar just outside of Philadelphia. I looked across the room and saw some people from the church my dad used to pastor. The father of the family came over to see how I was doing. He talked to me for a few minutes, but I think he could tell I was horribly bitter and that I wanted nothing to do with God or Christians.

I have to say, looking back, I'm proud of him because he got to the moment where he could have turned away and left. I believe he knew he was supposed to tell me God loved me. The brave soul went for it and said, "Jeremy, how are you doing with God?"

I got so angry when he said those words. I was bitter towards Christians and anything they had to say to me. I looked at him with the best death stare I could muster, held up my beer, pointed at it and said, "This is my God."

I totally disrespected the God of heaven by doing that. It was not a good moment for me. How beyond belief that He would forgive me and *still love me.*

God's Favorite

My Father in heaven loves me more than words can say. I'm His favorite, you know. Even though I disrespected Him and rejected Him – even with all that – God sent His only son to die for me. The Bible says I was a "stranger to God" and yet His son suffered the most painful death for me (Matthew 25:31-46).

I don't know about you, but if someone close to me was involved in something I hated, and on top of that, disrespected me and rejected me repeatedly – could I forgive? I have three children, and I wouldn't sacrifice the life of any one of them for a guy like that. Yet God, my Father in heaven, did this for me. He forgave me for all the things I did, then He adopted me and accepted me into His family. Jesus, His son, experienced a horrible death for someone who hated Him: Me. He did this because He loves me and I'm His favorite. Just as I always knew I was Grandpa's favorite, I now know I'm God's favorite.

You're His Favorite Too

I have good news for you. You are His favorite as well. No matter what you've done or said, He still loves you. Right now, He's whispering to your heart, saying:

> *"I love you so much. You are my favorite and I am proud of you. I want what is best for you. Trust in me to give you the desires of your heart."*

When you are coming out of your rut, many hard things will come your way. People who are used to you learning the hard way will talk bad about you and not believe in you. All kinds of surprises will come. But I want you to remember one thing through all of it. Keep your head up because you are God's favorite.

Remember how Grandpa made sure my special song was played for me every time I walked into his restaurant/

bar? God does the very same thing! He sees you as His favorite. In Zephaniah, the Bible says, "God sings a happy song over you" (Zephaniah 3:17). God has a special song just for you.

If you will always remember that you are God's favorite, I promise it will help you in your journey out of the rut of your destructive lifestyle.

It's in There

My Favorite Commercials

I had two favorite television commercials when I was growing up. The first was the old lady in the fast food commercial who, after receiving her hamburger order, looked at it and then back at the clerk, exclaiming, "Where's the beef?"

I died laughing every time I saw that thing. I walked around saying, "Where's the beef?"

(I do find weird things very funny. This may be why I am always the last one laughing at my jokes. The sad part is that most of the time, I'm still laughing beyond anyone else. Annie tells me no one actually laughs at my jokes – they laugh at me laughing at my own jokes.)

My other favorite television commercial when I was growing up starred a mother who was cooking pasta. Her family members would come into the kitchen and remind her to put certain ingredients into the sauce. Her reply was always the same: "It's in there."

I don't know why I found this so funny but I did. Maybe it's because I love one-liners and I love pasta.

I think they should bring the pasta commercial back again. First, because it's so funny, and second, because I want it to remind you of this book.

In *The Hard Way,* I have done my best to share what I see as the steps I have taken to get out of my rut. I am by no means perfect; I'm still very much a work in progress. But it has been many years since I cried out those gut-wrenching words, "My life Sucks!" My life doesn't suck now.

I pray that my story helps you find your way there too. I've said it many times – the only reason my story would be worth all the pain, is if other people learn from my mistakes and avoid having to learn the hard way by hitting rock bottom in their rut.

Sarah's Graduation Message

A few years ago, I was sitting in my sister Sarah's graduation ceremony. At that time, I was still in the mess of the rut I had put myself in. In that ceremony, I heard my sister give an amazing speech. She is a phenomenal writer and speaker. As she continued through her powerful speech, she came to the point where she thanked me, her older brother.

She said something to this effect: "I want to thank my big brother, Jeremy. Because of him, I have been known as

Jeremy's little sister my entire life. Also, because of him, I know many things *not to do* so I can avoid a lot of pain coming into my adult years."

Of course, she worded it more eloquently than this. To some, it may have sounded like an insult, but I didn't see it that way. In fact, it almost made me cry when I heard it. I was thankful that my story, my life, might help my sister avoid the pain I went through. I don't want anyone to have to learn the hard way.

Again, this is the whole reason for this book. I have poured my heart into this book. I have carefully outlined everything it took for me to get out of that rut. Just as the pasta sauce commercial states, "It's in there."

Every ingredient in any homemade pasta sauce is in there for a reason. If you know anything about specialty cooking, you know that if an ingredient is missing, the end product will not be as good, especially with pasta sauce.

I was blessed to grow up in a part of the country where Italian food was very popular. I'm talking about *authentic* Italian food. If you go to Philadelphia, you won't have to go far to find great Italian food. To this day I would prefer to go to the Italian Market at 9th and Washington over going to Disney World.

It's a Climbing Process

Authentic Italian pasta sauce just isn't right without the correct amount of every ingredient stirred in. It's important to know, "It's in there."

That's how I feel about this book. You may need to go back and re-read to fully understand every step. I put them in order so you can do each one as you are ready.

It's a climbing process; and each step takes you higher than the previous step. In this way, you can – through the process – reach the top and find a *life alive.* No matter where you are or what you need, "It's in there."

It's a climbing process; and each step takes you higher than the previous step.

Every journey is unique and there will be some steps in your journey you will have to take that I can't tell you about, because I don't know them. These will be steps that are unique to your personal journey.

Likewise, there were steps I took that I didn't put in this book because they seemed unique to me. What I did include are the main ingredients to help get you out of your rut, ingredients that can keep you from learning the hard way.

Time to Stew, Simmer and Internalize

Another thing about authentic pasta sauce is that it has to stew and simmer for a long time. I pray you will take these principles and concepts and stew on them for days. Think about them; internalize them; consume them. Make them part of your life.

Reviewing the Steps

Let's quickly go though the steps that will bring you up out of your rut (open-ended grave) and back into the land of the living.

The Diagnosis

Those who spend a lifetime of learning the hard way become experts at hiding from the truth. The first step is to get honest enough to diagnosis the problem.

The Father's Love

Coming to the realization that your Father-God loves you, and that He loves you right where you are (mess and all) will revolutionize your life.

Healing from the Past

As I stated, it's easy sometime to hide from the truth. That includes deep wounds from the past. Most of us are hurting people with deep issues. I had to drop the mask and admit that I was deeply hurt.

Every Tree Has a Root

Those who are in a destructive lifestyle don't just all of a sudden decide to live that way. Events and circumstances from the past trigger adverse behavior patterns. The next step is to get to the root cause of the problem.

Climbing Out of the Rut

In the journey to get out of the rut, oftentimes drastic decisions must be made and drastic actions must be taken.

I've Got Your Back

Don't try to go it alone. You will definitely need God's help; you will also need God's people. Surround yourself with those who love you, who support you, who believe in you.

Transparency Matters

By now you've admitted you have a problem, and you've stopped pretending. Are there still more things in your past that need to be brought to the light?

Do They Think You're Crazy Yet?

Friends from your old life, from your past, will not understand your new life. They think you're crazy. It doesn't matter what they think. It only matters what God thinks!

Emotions vs. Emotional

Emotions are God-given, but you need not be ruled by your emotions. Learn to control your emotions, and you will stand stronger than ever before.

12 Days Is Longer than 12 Years

The first days when coming out of the rut will absolutely be the most difficult. They will seem an eternity. With God's help and with the help of your new support team, you can do it!

Detox

Detoxing is more than drying out from alcohol and drugs. It can be rest. True rest. Resting in the Lord and trusting Him. Anything of quality in a person's life always takes more than a day to accomplish. Anything worth having takes time and effort.

Risk for the Good

Those in a destructive lifestyle will risk their lives to get another fix. They risk prison, and risk losing those closest to them. Coming out of the rut means you can still risk, but now you will *risk good*!

Helping Others Helps You

Learn the amazing magic that happens when you reach out to help others. It hastens the healing!

It's About Generations

Its' not all about you. There are generations to come who are looking to you and depending on you. Don't let them down.

Tortured

The tortured mind aspect of having lived a long time in a destructive lifestyle is real and valid. Know you are not alone; learn how to deal with it and win.

Small Beginnings

Coming out of the rut can often become an inch-by-inch process. Learn to celebrate the smallest achievements. Never despise the day of small beginnings.

Know Your Gift

Never underestimate the power of knowing your personal talents and giftings. I was a great salesman with strong leadership qualities; but used the wrong way only got me into trouble. Learn your gifts and use them for good.

Thanks Carter

A good friend named Carter, taught me that I should have at least three trades that would bring in a decent income. This, he insisted, would prevent being desperate for money and turn again to dealing drugs. It worked!

Never Quit

Failure doesn't mean you have to quit. If you fall, and you will, always get back up. Failure is never permanent until you quit. Don't quit!

You're His Favorite

Above all, remember that you are God's favorite! Believe it. Live it.

_____

Please let me know if my story has helped you. You are why I wrote it. Knowing others are being helped and getting healed is what this is all about.

I hope to hear your story. Remember, I'm cheering you on. I have given my life to pull people out of the rut that is similar to the one I was in. I am now, and will continue to be, your biggest cheerleader.

Don't go through the pain of the hard way. Leave your rut behind and live your dreams. Your life is a legacy that will impact generations.

Now take the ingredients of this book, *The Hard Way*,
and go live *life alive*.

Now take the ingredients of this book, *The Hard Way*, and go live *life alive*.

I would say good luck to you, but you don't need *luck*.

After all, you're God's favorite.

CPSIA information can be obtained at www.ICGtesting.com
Printed in the USA
LVOW060003250512

283240LV00003B/3/P